On page 51, the photographs of Toni Morrison
and Cornelia Bailey are misidentified.

The publisher and *Good Company*'s editor in chief,
Grace Bonney, regret and apologize for this error.

The photographs should appear as follows:

Toni Morrison

Cornelia Bailey

Editor's Letter

Have you ever dreamed of starting your own something? Maybe your own business? Have you ever imagined what it would feel like to turn your passion into a project that supports you? Have you ever pictured turning the key to the door of your first store or handing someone a business card with your name at the top?

You are in good company.

You are holding what I've always dreamed of creating. It's a magazine that is a conversation. It's a place for people in the creative community to connect, share, and learn together. Not just about ways to start and run businesses, but also about ways to live fuller, more meaningful lives and to find (and be) the support we all need to do our best.

This first issue is all about *community*. We'll look at the ways people within the creative world have banded together to create safe, supportive, and inspiring spaces. We'll look at how they're transforming representation in the media. And we'll talk openly about the importance of community health, both mental and physical.

In the stories that follow, you'll meet people who share your goals and aspirations—both big and small. They know what it feels like to dream big, overcome obstacles, and be vulnerable.

Good Company was inspired by a book I wrote called *In the Company of Women* that features over one hundred women who run their own creative practices and businesses, from painters and poets to heads of national corporations. *In the Company of Women* taught me that there are an infinite number of paths to success and each story is worth telling and listening to. It also taught me that nothing great is ever created alone. When we work together, we succeed.

Good Company continues the conversations started in that book. Here we'll discuss, in great depth and with honesty, the challenges and triumphs of work life.

Thank you for joining the conversation. I'm so happy to be in your company.

Love,

BE RELENTLESS

BE AMBITIOUS

BE EXCELLENT

—Roxane Gay

Contents

artwork by Robert & Stella

Contributors

We were so lucky to work with an incredible team of writers, artists, business owners, and activists to bring this first issue to life. Please follow their work online and off for more inspiration and motivation.

1 SHAUNA AHERN Shauna Ahern has been writing since she could hold a pen. She currently writes recipes for her much-loved website, Gluten-Free Girl, and for her upcoming book of essays, *Enough*. She lives on Vashon Island, in Washington State. She's either eating, laughing, or sleeping as you read this. glutenfreegirl.com @glutenfreegirl

2 HEATHER L. BARMORE Heather Barmore is a political communications professional who currently serves as the Director of Digital and Organizing Strategy for Planned Parenthood Affiliates of California. Her career in politics and activism started with an affinity for C-SPAN, particularly US Senate procedure. She believes in political engagement, storytelling, and dresses with pockets. @heatherbarmore

3 REBEKAH CAREY Rebekah Carey is an editor, stylist, and creative director. She currently lives in Berkeley, California, but her heart is never far from her native Oregon. She is passionate about social justice, small space design, adoption, budget-friendly creativity and design, and rescue dogs. aandbcreative.com @aandbcreative

4 GRACE D. CHIN Born in Hollywood, California, Grace D. Chin now proudly claims Lawrence, Kansas, as home. She holds a visual arts BFA (with an emphasis in printmaking) from the University of Kansas. Her favorite pastime is to gain increasingly impractical skills making things with paper. gracedchin.com @gracedchin

5 CHERYL DAY Cheryl Day is a James Beard–nominated baker and author specializing in Southern American baking. She is passionate about passing on the traditions of hospitality, community, and celebration, and preserving these recipes for future generations. She and husband Griffith established Back in the Day Bakery in Savannah, Georgia, in 2002 backinthedaybakery.com @starbrownie

6 NORA GOMEZ-STRAUSS By day Nora is Public Art Fund's Director of Digital Strategies. In her rare spare time she attempts to keep up with her photography. She currently lives in her native borough of Queens, New York, with her husband and son, where they enjoy going for long walks and listening to records. nogophoto.com @nogophoto

7 DAWN HANCOCK Dawn is a troublemaker, a bleeding heart, a designer by trade, and a do-gooder by choice. She started Firebelly in 1999 with a simple mission: Good Design for Good Reason. Since then, she's been diligent about hiring passionate people, seeking out fearless allies, and taking on projects to change the world. firebellydesign.com @firebellydesign

8 SASHA ISRAEL Sasha Israel is a portrait and lifestyle photographer who splits her time between New York City and Cambridge, Massachusetts. Sasha was the principal photographer for the *New York Times* bestseller *In the Company of Women*, and her work has been featured in publications such as *Vogue, Elle, Self,* and *Glamour.* sashaisraelphotography.com @sashaisrael

9 SHARLENE KING Sharlene is a designer in Chicago working on making financial tech more accessible. She moonlights as a corrupter of youth by mentoring students through the Adler Planetarium, Chicago Public Schools, and other mentorship programs. Her aloe plants keep having babies. tinytank.net @typodactyl

10 KAT KINSMAN Kat Kinsman is the author of *Hi, Anxiety: Life With a Bad Case of Nerves,* Senior Food and Drinks Editor at Time Inc.'s all-breakfast site Extra Crispy, and the founder of Chefs With Issues. tart.org @kittenwithawhip

11 AVERY KUA Avery is a freelance illustrator and snake enthusiast based in Toronto who is juggling life and three start-ups—two of which are hers, one of which she started with her boyfriend. Even though she loves drawing, she doesn't usually draw for fun. She's currently looking forward to getting adult braces. averykua.com @avrykua

12

13

14

15

12 LOSTBOY Lostboy is a queer first-generation Korean American artist whose work spans identity, connections, community, and desire. She has had the honor of having her drawings appear with/in Lady Gaga, Samsung, Planned Parenthood, the *New York Times,* and many more. lostboyillustrations.com @lostboyillustrations

13 KRYSTAL MACK Krystal Mack is a writer and recipe developer from Baltimore, Maryland. She is the founder of BLK//SUGAR, BLK//MARKET, and KarmaPop. @krystalcmack *Headshot credit: Dave Cooper.*

14 KLANCY MILLER Klancy Miller is the author of *Cooking Solo: The Fun of Cooking for Yourself.* She studied patisserie at Le Cordon Bleu in Paris and appeared on Food Network's *Recipe for Success* and Cooking Channel's *Unique Sweets.* She has contributed to *Cherry Bombe, Bon Appétit,* the *Washington Post, Food52,* and *Food Republic.* klancymiller.com @klancycooks

15 MIMI POND Mimi Pond is a cartoonist and writer whose two recent graphic novels, *Over Easy* and *The Customer Is Always Wrong,* were published by Drawn and Quarterly. A contributor to *The New Yorker,* she lives in Los Angeles. mimipond.com

16

17

18

19

16 AREEBA SIDDIQUE Areeba Siddique is an artist from Pakistan. Currently on her gap year, she's trying to make the internet a Muslim women–friendly place. @ohareeba

17 MIRIAM KLEIN STAHL Miriam Klein Stahl is a Bay Area artist, educator, and activist, and the *New York Times*–bestselling illustrator of *Rad American Women A–Z* and *Rad Women Worldwide*. She follows in a tradition of making socially relevant works. As an educator, she has dedicated her teaching practice to addressing equity through the lens of the arts. Stahl's most recent project is a skateboard company called Pave the Way. miriamkleinstahl.com

18 EMMA STRAUB Emma Straub is a *New York Times*–bestselling novelist and the owner of Books Are Magic, an independent bookstore in Brooklyn, New York. booksaremagic.net @emmastraub

19 REBEKAH G. TAUSSIG Rebekah Taussig is a Kansas City writer and teacher with a PhD in creative nonfiction and disability studies. Her writing contributes to the collective narratives being told about disability—empowering, mundane, wild, heartbreaking, exhilarating, ordinary stories of her life lived through a paralyzed body. rebekahtaussig.com @sitting_pretty

20 NICOLE A. TAYLOR Nicole is a multimedia storyteller and author of *The Up South Cookbook*. She has contributed to the *New York Times, Saveur, SheKnows, The Undefeated, The Bitter Southerner,* and *Civil Eats* and hosted the "Hot Grease" podcast on Heritage Radio Network. Taylor founded *The Modern Travelers' Green Zine* and edited recipes for *Crop Stories: Sweet Potatoes.* She lives in Brooklyn, New York. foodculturist.com @foodculturist

21 JULIA TURSHEN Julia Turshen is the bestselling author of *Feed the Resistance* and *Small Victories*. She has also written for the *New York Times,* the *Washington Post,* the *Wall Street Journal, Vogue, Bon Appétit, Food & Wine,* and *Saveur.* She lives in New York's Hudson Valley with her wife and their dogs and cat. juliaturshen.com @turshen

22 LOVEIS WISE Loveis Wise is a Capricorn lady from Washington, DC—now drawing in Philadelphia. She enjoys illustrating plants and women doing cool things in everyday life. loveiswise.com @cosmicsomething

23 MEGAN WOOD Megan Wood co-founded 44 North Coffee in Deer Isle, Maine. A native Mainer, Wood has worked with nonprofit organizations and outdoor industries, and as an artist's assistant. She is fascinated by what creates community and where nature intersects and inspires human interaction. Her personal goal: see the sunrise and stars and swim in the sea, daily. 44northcoffee.com @medewo

What does community mean to you?

by Klancy Miller

illustrations by Avery Kua

Community. At its best, it supports you, reflects who you are, it inspires you. You're born into one and you may choose several others. I spoke with five powerful women—Jodie Patterson, social activist, writer, and entrepreneur; Tavi Gevinson, writer, actor, and founder of *Rookie*; Melissa King, chef; Tanya Aguiñiga, furniture designer/maker; and Marianna Martinelli, Director of Community at The Wing—to learn their definition of community and how it influences the way they work and live.

MELISSA KING: Community is my place of belonging and acceptance. It's a place where we can gather to explore new ideas, talk about old ones, support one another, and work toward common goals.

JODIE PATTERSON: I used to think my community was the black community. I've always felt racially, culturally, historically connected to all black people anywhere and everywhere. My parents knew how small a little black girl could feel in a white, male-dominated world, so they put me at the center and subsequently I grew to feel like a warrior. And then when I had a child that I understood to be transgender, and when the world I knew didn't incorporate or support him or place him at the center of things, I quickly and swiftly widened my community to include LGBTQI folks. My community now is anyone who is of, and supports, that which is most important to me: black, female, and queer.

TANYA AGUIÑIGA: Community means getting to know other people and other people knowing you. It means knowing what is important to you and having others make space for things that are important to you.

MARIANNA MARTINELLI: It's a shared value set and it's a group of people working toward a shared ideal. And that can look like a lot of things.

TAVI GEVINSON: I'm lucky to have communities in all of the different industries I'm in. I'm close to the people I did a play with and I'm also close to the community at *Rookie*—there's a strong sense of a shared worldview. That's what makes both industries bearable.

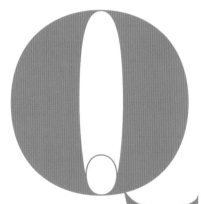

When did you first experience the importance of community?

MELISSA KING: I first experienced community in a restaurant. Restaurants are made up of people from all walks of life with a range of skills and talents. Everything in a restaurant is orchestrated and dependent on each team member's performance. Everyone is vital. A restaurant thrives best when we can look beyond gender, social class, sexual orientation, and color to create an accepting community working toward the core goals of hospitality.

TANYA AGUIÑIGA: I started doing community-based work in 1997. I was involved in the Border Art Workshop and we worked on human rights issues. We worked with a community on the outskirts of my town and that's when I learned how to collaborate with others and how to work as a team toward a larger goal. It's about knowing that there's a bigger picture and that you as an individual are not at the center of the universe.

MARIANNA MARTINELLI: I'm from a small homogenous community in Texas. People looked out for each other, knew each other's kids. It was a very narrow view of the world, but that was sort of my introduction to community.

TAVI GEVINSON: I started my blog when I was eleven. A friend of mine from community theater had a sister with a fashion blog and I wanted in. I knew online there would be a cool big sister community and they would get what I was trying to do.

MELISSA KING: It's expanded beyond just cooking. I've been looking outside of the culinary community and into others that might overlap—music, art, film, health, and technology. I want to work with people in other areas to influence our communities for the better. I look at all the communities I proudly represent— women of color, LGBTQ, female chefs, entrepreneurs, Californian, etc. I'm fortunate to be in a position today where I can have a voice for those who may not.

TANYA AGUIÑIGA: I have a larger sense of community now. I recognize all the different things that encompass my identity and that I'm part of a lot of communities, not just based on my region but also based on my ethnicity, my gender, my life experiences, and all of the different things that make up who I am.

How has your sense of community changed over the years as your career/business has grown?

MARIANNA MARTINELLI: New York has opened my mind to community as a whole. New Yorkers get a bad reputation for being out for themselves, but I think people who live here are really community minded because they realize you can't do everything by yourself.

TAVI GEVINSON: Your real-life community is sacred. So many industries are social, but they're like a hall of mirrors. There can be fake bonding and false intimacy that I react poorly to. So my sense of community has shifted. You don't need to be liked by thousands of people. You need three really good friends and put those friendships first.

TANYA AGUIÑIGA: My community brings different perspectives into my everyday life. All the people who work in my studio are from different cultural backgrounds. That helps me understand perspectives outside of my own and how we can work toward a greater sense of unity. I am constantly shifting the way we work so we can make space for different methodologies and technical abilities and make sure that everybody feels empowered and has an equal voice.

MELISSA KING: I represent several minority communities and try to find ways to collaborate with these communities to create something new to share with the world. I have organized pop-up dinners with female *Top Chef* contestants to benefit La Cocina (an organization that supports low-income female food entrepreneurs) and I've collaborated with Humphry Slocombe, a local San Francisco ice cream company, to create a Hong Kong Milk Tea ice cream inspired by my Chinese background. I'm proud to be able to use food as a platform to represent my communities.

How does your community influence the way you work?

TAVI GEVINSON: I will send my friends ten pages of what I'm writing. And they'll send pages one to twenty-five. There's ongoing emotional support. Things like that help.

JODIE PATTERSON: I work for my community as a writer, an activist, and a thoughtful parent. Even the work I do at my kids' school is for the betterment of our community. As an author and an activist, I use words and stories to help change bias. As a parent, I teach my kids to be flexible. We need more intellectual dexterity in order to unite with people from all walks of life. We need to put ideas on the table, test them out, talk them through, and see where we can learn.

MELISSA KING: Online and offline, I just try to continue being myself. On social media I openly share photos of me and my girlfriend at a Pride parade or in a kitchen working with other badass female chefs. These are all real moments in my life that I feel sharing can help to open up dialogue or make someone out there feel they can relate and be a part of my community.

MARIANNA MARTINELLI: We've been lucky to connect with a lot of people from diverse backgrounds and diverse points of view on Instagram. Our content there has resonated with people who feel angry, hurt, or marginalized and we work hard to create a digital safe place to commiserate, vent, and talk.

How have you created a sense of community online and offline?

TANYA AGUIÑIGA: In real life it's mainly about talking to people, and getting to know them. I try to get to know my neighbors, step back from my own narrative, and learn how I can support them and in their work. Online I try to post and give people more of an insight into my personal narrative so they get to know a little bit more about where I'm coming from, where the studio is coming from, and everybody who works in the studio. Giving people more insight into our lives, more perspective, and a little more content helps people feel like they're connected to other humans rather than just to products.

TWO GENERATIONS OF BUSINESS OWNERS

CHERYL DAY

KRYSTAL MACK

TALK SHOP

Veteran baker Cheryl Day of Back in the Day Bakery in Savannah, Georgia, has been in the business since 2002, bringing delicious traditional baked goods to her customers, with the help of her husband and co-baker, Griffith Day.

Baker Krystal Mack of BLK// SUGAR opened her first brick-and-mortar location in 2016 in her hometown of Baltimore, Maryland. Mack recently closed her shop to evolve the business toward a thoroughly modern model of online selling, with deliveries coming from wholesale, social media, and Uber Eats.

lettering by Annica Lyndenberg

Both bakeries are beloved by their clientele and both Cheryl and Krystal have a devoted following that admires not just their delicious sweets, but also the business ethos behind them. So they sat down together to see how their paths have been similar (and different) and to discuss the lessons they've learned at each of their stages of life and business.

Is there a quotation or saying that inspires you and motivates you to be yourself and do what you love?

CHERYL: Maya Angelou's quote "I've learned that people will forget what you said, people will forget what you did, but people will never forget how you made them feel." This quote always inspires me to create a lovely experience for all who visit our bakery.

KRYSTAL: I love Maya Angelou! Have you ever read her cookbooks? She is a major hero of mine and I have a photo of her at my desk. Such an inspiration! My quote is rather long, but it comes from *The Prophet* by Kahlil Gibran. "Always you have been told that work is a curse and labor a misfortune. But I say to you that when you work you fulfill a part of earth's furthest dream, assigned to you when that dream was born. And in keeping yourself with labor you are in truth loving life. And to love life through labor is to be intimate with life's inmost secret." That quote reminds me why what I am doing is so special. While work is most often fun, it can at times be a bit draining. That's when I think of that quote and remember that I am fortunate to be doing what I love for a living and that what I do can be enjoyed by others.

What is the characteristic about yourself you're proudest of?

CHERYL: I have been told that I am a trailblazer and I have a knack for spotting trends.

KRYSTAL: My ability to be up front and open with others. I've found that it has really helped keep my personal and professional relationships meaningful as well as allowed them to grow and thrive.

What was the inspiration/reason for starting your company?

CHERYL: The inspiration for starting Back in the Day Bakery was to do something I am passionate about and to live a creative life. I wanted to re-create the feeling of visiting neighborhood bakeries from my childhood growing up in Los Angeles; to build a business that supported a community and help revitalize a Savannah neighborhood and help it thrive again.

KRYSTAL: When I started BLK//SUGAR, it came out of wanting to continue on my creative path, grow in my love of baking, and also just be stable and fulfilled. I guess I just wanted to live my "best life" and inspire others to do the same. Over time my purpose evolved and now I feel BLK//SUGAR is filling the void of young black female bakers and owners in the food scene. I often try to incorporate representation and feminism into the work we do and organizations we support because I want to build more meaning into my work. As a worker/owner I always wanted to try and make a difference as much as I can. For me it's natural to do this through my business because that is really all I have time for and I think it makes the combined effort of advocacy, business, and activism more impactful.

What is a day in the life of your job like?

CHERYL: Nearly sixteen years in—and I am still very hands on in the daily operations of Back in the Day Bakery. Most days we put the key in the bakery door at 4 a.m. (earlier during holiday season) and I am at the bakery until about 5 p.m. (even later if we have a community event). I spend the wee hours of the morning baking with my team, but most of my time is spent ensuring a positive customer experience in every way I can. I spend my evenings studying and researching my craft and the history of Southern baking, and I am currently writing my third cookbook on this subject.

Owning a business makes you very resilient and you have to learn to bounce back from just about anything you can imagine. —*Cheryl*

KRYSTAL: For me my days vary depending on orders. We have a number of wholesale accounts in the Baltimore area so I'm up at 3 to 4 a.m. on weekdays baking for orders. Then it's off to make deliveries. I also spend my time scheduling CTAs (calls to action or content that will drive dessert sales, ticket sales, etc.) for the weeks ahead, going over my production schedule, organizing invoices, and preparing for catering orders. I also try to schedule one to two days a week to build content for our website. That could be anything from checking out the thriving food scene in Baltimore to meeting a local maker or artisan for an interview.

What is the thing you're proudest of that you (or the company as a whole) have done so far?

CHERYL: I am proud of everything we have accomplished as a small business independently without the help of any investors. We are not only self-taught bakers but we are also self-taught business owners who have kept our business open even after enduring many obstacles. We have had many high moments of our careers—like writing two successful cookbooks and our James Beard nomination and creating a Savannah food landmark—but honestly if I had to choose one thing that I am proudest of, I would say the fact that we have been able to provide a living wage for our team to be able to live their dreams while they are helping us to live ours.

KRYSTAL: I'm most proud of the feedback that I have gotten from customers and admirers of BLK//SUGAR about the fact that I take a stance on current political and social events. It's a risky approach to running a business, but I often get emails from customers saying how they respect and appreciate the bakery's values. It reminds me that there is nothing wrong with staying true to what matters to you while also doing what you love. I will also say that another proud moment is being able to have opportunities like these to reflect and share what I've learned on my journey. It gives me pride knowing that people can save themselves some stress and heartache from hearing about my journey thus far.

How did you come up with your business's aesthetic and what inspires it?

CHERYL: Back in the Day Bakery is the most authentic representation of myself. I have been inspired by the history of the American South and vintage treasures for as long as I can remember. I collect vintage portraits and African American art and much of my collection graces the walls at the bakery. I went to flea markets with my mother growing up and I wanted the bakery to have a very comfortable, collected kind of feeling that would make folks that were already living in the neighborhood as comfortable as those who visit us from afar.

KRYSTAL: The aesthetic for BLK//SUGAR was inspired by contemporary bakehouses on the West Coast, but also my own personal style. The colors of the logo are black and pink. When I was a kid, this particular shade of pink was my favorite color. It's kind of a Pepto-Bismol pink. As an adult, my favorite color is black. I felt the two forward slashes between "BLK" and "SUGAR" added a contemporary touch. I often like to think beyond logos when it comes to brand development. I wanted the name of the bakery itself to be memorable. To me the bakery is a representation of me as a black woman. We had all kinds of work from women and black artists on the wall, beautiful trailing philodendrons, and marble and glass cake stands and displays for our baked goods. All in all I would say our aesthetic is inspired by my take on the contemporary black woman.

WELCOME

TO

BACK IN THE DAY BAKERY

WE HANDCRAFT EVERYTHING
FROM SCRATCH AND IT'S
MADE WITH LOVE!

SLOW DOWN & TASTE THE SWEET LIFE

EATS

·SPECIALTY SANDWICHES·

COOL

SUPER CHICKEN 8.95
JAMBON & TALLEGIO 8.95
CURRY CHICKEN 8.95
GEORGETTE 8.95
ROSEMARY CHICKEN 8.95

HOT

BACON & ONION 9.75
PIMENTO & PIG 8.95
GRILLED CHEESE 6.50
HAM & FONTINA 8.25

VEGETARIAN

FARMWICH 8.95 | CAPRESE 8.95

HAPPY DAY SALAD 10.00

D

LATTE
CAPPUC
MOCHA
AMERI
ESPRES
COFFEE
ICED CO
MONDO B

SOY - 1
EXTRA SH

There is nothing wrong with staying true to what matters to you while also doing what you love. —Krystal

What brands or businesses do you admire?

CHERYL: I am inspired by brands that are authentic and have built a creative and caring culture in an approachable way. I admire Star Provisions, Jeni's Splendid Ice Creams, Hedley and Bennett, and Glossier.

KRYSTAL: I'm inspired by brands that have a distinct voice. I'm really impressed by what Chloe Coscarelli and her team have done at By Chloe. I also really admire the following that Moon Juice has built. As a whole, I love what Solange Knowles has done with Saint Heron and what Kai Avent-deLeon has done with Sincerely, Tommy and S, T Coffee.

What have been the biggest challenges of starting/running your business so far, and what are you doing to overcome them?

CHERYL: Staffing. Finding talented bakers who are dedicated to the craft of baking and willing to take the long road to learning and growing. It is difficult dealing with real-life obstacles and running a business at the same time. Owning a business makes you very resilient and you have to learn to bounce back from just about anything you can imagine.

I am overcoming this challenge by casting a wider net to find people that want to be a part of the culture that we have created at our bakery. I realized that I have something positive to offer and I have learned to be patient. Also, when things don't work out, I have learned to recognize this sooner rather than later.

KRYSTAL: I would say the biggest challenge that I have faced so far is discernment when it comes to hiring. I learned early on that hiring friends is not the way to go, but I often find myself holding on to employees who are underperforming or not at all a good fit just because they are great people. I think that the best way to overcome that is by trusting my intuition as a business owner. It's something that is new to me, but I just have to trust my judgment and remember that the future of my business relies on that.

What was the best piece of business advice you were given when you started?

CHERYL: My sister was an incurable entrepreneur and she taught me many of my most valued lessons in business and in life. She told me to always be consistent. In the early days when business was slow in the late afternoons and I had already worked a long day, it was tempting to hang the "gone fishing" sign, but I always remembered her words.

I think it is fantastic advice for both the start-up and the established business owner to not rest on your laurels. Whether it is the hours you are open for business or the frequency in posting on a blog, let people know they can depend on you. In our business, I believe that being consistent has been one of the best ways to build our reputation and to grow our business.

KRYSTAL: The best piece of advice I received was to do this for me and not anyone else. It sounds simple enough, but it's easy to forget when customers give menu suggestions or may not necessarily agree with a change we make. You want to make everyone happy, but I have to also remember that not everyone is going to be into what we do and that is okay.

If you could hire a dream employee to help with *one* thing, what would you need or want help with most?

CHERYL: My dream employee is someone who gets as excited about putting the key in the bakery door as my husband and I do. Someone dependable whom I could trust and who would help with the daily operations of running the business and helping it grow.

KRYSTAL: A dream marketing assistant! That would leave more time for me to bake (what I love to do the most). They would have a true understanding of the voice of my brand, be great at social media, graphics, and photography, and also find a way to schedule CTAs.

What are the top three things someone should consider before starting their own business?

CHERYL: Do you have a story to tell? Are you ready to work really, really hard to follow your dream? Are you doing it for love or money?

I would suggest immersing yourself in the culture of your trade in any way you can. Seek out a mentorship or apprenticeship and/or join professional organizations (and don't forget to learn the business side of things, too!). I think it is important to take an honest look at yourself and what it takes to be successful in your field of interest.

KRYSTAL: Remember why you are starting. The further you progress, it can be difficult to remember the "why." When you forget that, work becomes less fun and you can become stagnant in reaching whatever goals you initially set starting out. When that happens, is it really worth continuing to invest your time and effort?

Looking back, what do you wish you'd known about running a business?

CHERYL: The advice I wish I had been given early on was to stay focused. Don't think you have to be everything to everybody. Come up with a plan and stick to it no matter what anyone says. Folks will run you into the ground if you let them.

KRYSTAL: I wish I'd known how competitive it can be. While I find what we do at the bakery to be equally traditional and unique, there are always imitators and people trying to outdo something original to our brand. While I take most things as a compliment, I also see it as a reminder to constantly be innovative and not get too comfortable doing the same old things.

What are your goals going forward or next steps you'd like to take as a brand?

CHERYL: Our goal is to continue to teach the craft of Southern baking and to continue our mission of creating great food at our bakery. We are working toward this goal by continuing to write cookbooks as well as exploring other media outlets such as product development and television.

KRYSTAL: My short-term goal is to continue to increase our wholesale accounts. My personal short-term goal is to get back into writing. This could be in the form of journaling for myself as well as for more online and print publications. Every time I see Dr. Jessica B. Harris, she always asks me if I've started journaling consistently and I'm always ashamed to say, "No, I have not." I owe it to my future self to have something to look back on at such a crazy and exciting time in my life. Long term, I want to bring more national attention to Baltimore and its growing food and arts scene. Hopefully that will provide our creatives with more opportunities.

Cheryl, what is one thing you want newer businesses owners to know?

CHERYL: That dedication is the key to success.

Krystal, what is one thing you want longtime business owners to know?

KRYSTAL: That it's never too late to pivot or switch things up a bit. Sometimes it refreshes perspective and keeps your dedicated following on their toes.

Cheryl, what is one thing you've learned from newer business owners like Krystal?

CHERYL: I have learned the importance of creating a visual social media presence to reach a broader network in my industry and beyond, making connections with folks all over the globe.

Krystal, what is something important you've learned from longtime business owners like Cheryl?

KRYSTAL: To stay the course and not give up easily. And to build community with others in the industry in your city. We are stronger when united.

FINDING

COMMUNITY

ONLINE

AND OFF

by Shauna Ahern

This was back before an industry had grown up around blogs, like parapets around the heart of the castle. In 2005, there was no Twitter, Facebook, Snapchat, or Instagram. No one entertained the expectation that money could be made by posting recipes online or sharing design ideas. We were just sharing what we loved.

In the winter of 2005, I lay ill, sleeping most of the day, in pain, leaving the house only for the latest medical appointment. Save for the help of a clutch of close friends and my family, I felt alone in this. No one understood what was happening with my body. No doctor had a diagnosis. After every MRI or ultrasound, I crawled back onto my couch. So, when I was diagnosed with celiac disease in April of 2005, I rejoiced. I knew what was wrong with me. And I could fix it, merely by eating great food that happened to not contain gluten? Hurrah!

My natural inclination was to say yes to this. Why linger on the disappointment of never being able to eat a croissant again? I felt well again. That tasted better than layers of butter and flour ever could. And immediately, I began to write. As a child, as soon as I understood that it was humans who wrote books, and not some magic force, I wanted to write one. After a week of going without gluten, I knew what I needed to do. I started cooking. I took photographs of what I cooked. And I wrote stories. A friend dubbed me the Gluten-Free Girl. My brother told me

about a service called Blogspot. Always fascinated by new technology, I liked the idea of typing something online, instead of the words staying hidden in my journal. I began writing and sent the link to friends across the country. I wrote every day for weeks, exulting in my resurging energy.

One morning, I turned on the computer and found a comment from a stranger. If I had begun a food blog five years later, I might have seen that comment as a confirmation of my expectations of success. Instead, I stared at it and thought, *Who the heck is this?* Without intending to, I had begun one of the first gluten-free food blogs in the world. People who googled "gluten-free recipes" six weeks after I began writing found my site.

This is how my online community began.

That first comment tumbled into a slew of comments and became a regular group of people who returned. Because social media did not exist yet, all conversation happened in the comments sections. And I believe that the fact that I was not making money from this made the comments a joy, a true conversation in community. All of us gluten-free people were simply happy to know we were not alone. After one year, I met my husband, the Chef, as I called him then. Women around the world wrote to me to say they loved our story and they were hoping for one like it, too. I met my husband at thirty-nine. Convinced that I would never meet someone who would love my bookish enthusiasms, my love of food, my age and relative inexperience in romance, I flung myself fully into my work and met him through it. I'm still amazed.

Shauna with her husband, Danny, and their son, Desmond.

For years, Gluten-Free Girl brought joy. It was a lark, a happy experiment of a place where I could play with boozy Fig Newtons, roasted chicken thighs with a sauce made of Scotch, and stories of spilling stock on myself and laughing. I poured out my stories. People kept coming. And there I was, with a husband who created recipes with me, and thousands of women and men cheering us on loudly. I was the happiest I had ever been in my life. For the first time in my life, I did not feel lonely.

Our daughter was born. And the community sent thousands of comments and emails to us, praying for her when she was in the NICU, sighing with relief when she came home. We felt held in the scariest place of our lives. It still astounds me, that love.

How different it feels now.

Fast-forward, in a rapid-shift montage, to 2015, a decade after I began writing my site. Twitter launched. Facebook came into people's homes. Bloggers started receiving cookbook deals, including me and Danny. Ad networks sprang up. Suddenly, the idea of long, interesting comments on blogs was no longer the metric of success. I stopped enjoying it as much. There were many moments of connection still: the women who wrote to say I had given them hope when they made pancakes everyone liked; the heartfelt letters from people who had been reading from the early days and still stayed. I started a file on my laptop labeled "Read this." They were comments that reminded me why I did all this. Meanwhile, I tried to come up with a video strategy for our work, watched endless YouTube videos on every new technological task I had to master to move forward, and tried to pretend I knew what I was doing.

I spent most of my days up on the parapets, by myself, trying to defend the castle. I rarely had the chance to go into the castle, sit in front of the fire, and simply rest.

Shauna and her friends meet for dinner at their home on Vashon Island in Washington.

In the spring of 2015, I stood looking out the window of the kitchen studio we were renting at the time. We thought we needed a place to hold dinners, to test our recipes for cookbooks, to seem more professional than we felt. I had a day of meetings about the gluten-free flour we were bringing to market. The friend who was helping us with our business had been pushing us to come up with our next five intellectual property deals. There were conversations about package redesigns and Amazon sales and whether or not we could take out a loan to bring out the grain-free blend. Everyone had left for the day. I was alone, staring out at the twilight sky. And the thought occurred to me, fully formed: I guess I'm not a writer anymore. There was no time to write. I would have to let it go.

A month later, I had a minor stroke. It terrified me. It also caused me to realign my life. Over the next two years, my husband and I let go of our flour business. We decided to take some time off before we pursued another cookbook deal. We stopped renting that studio. I started writing again.

And whenever my husband and I talked, as we did endlessly for months, about what had changed and from where our happiness comes, we realized it always came back to the same three things. He wants to cook. I want to write. Together, we want to create community. Everything else was a distraction.

I let go of writing on Gluten-Free Girl on a regular basis, only updating when it felt right. We let go of the notion that we would ever make money through our website. And we started working in our town instead. We live on a rural island off Seattle, a funky, wonderful small town, full of artists, activists, and men in John Deere caps. In all those years of pursuing more followers, more hits on the website, and more book sales, we hardly lived in our own town. We determined to change that.

Now, twelve years after I read that first comment on my site, I no longer publish comments. I write when I feel the urge to share something and let it go into the world instead of looking for confirmation. I'm working on a book of essays that has nothing to do with food. And the rest of the time? Danny is making food for people on Vashon, in their homes instead of in restaurants. He drives a big truck once a week to pick up food in Seattle for the island food bank. I'm on the program committee for the food bank. We have a group of friends we adore, all of whom love food, their kids, and the absurdities of life. We gather at the table together to eat, to share stories, to feel like we belong to each other. Instead of trying to document those meals and share them with the world, I leave my phone upstairs. We're laughing now, every day.

Sharing stories online is the work I do from 9 to 5. I take the weekends off from work and spend the time with my family and friends, the celebrations of a small town that fill me with such joy. I'm here now.

And I'm not alone at all.

He wants to cook. I want to write. Together, we want to create community.

While many shops remain unchanged over the decades, the prevalence and popularity of tattooing has only grown. Shops have rituals and unspoken codes of conduct that govern everything from how an apprentice is hired to how to handle a malodorous client.

As individuals, our reasons for getting tattoos will be as varied as the art itself, and our artists will have to follow or get left behind. Communities are often built by those who can adapt, not those who refuse. When I asked Tine DeFiore how to succeed in tattooing, she said this: "You work hard and put your mind to it. It's a lifestyle, but it's also a career, and it's what I want to do all day every day. It's so much more than work."

---

by Sharlene King

For the past eighteen years, I've been collecting tattoos as a way to feel like I've had control over something during a precarious time in my life. They're hidden when I visit my mom in contrast to more socially acceptable accomplishments. I handed her a framed copy of my college diploma dressed in business casual.

The desire to control how the world perceives us is a part of us all; however, the tattoo industry has always been male dominated and attached to specific social stigmas from class to criminality. Despite the popularity of tattoos today (and my mom's access to photos of me in T-shirts), I still can't bring myself to bridge that gap.

The four shops profiled know my experience all too well. In their own ways, they're trying to change the community with their art. They want all women to feel heard and be able to remember their own voice on their body.

Black Oak Tattoo, Chicago

'm standing outside Black Oak Tattoo in Chicago looking to talk with shop owner Tine DeFiore. "Knock if doorbell doesn't work," the door says. I step back to look for the street address, when a head pops out the door and asks over the dulcet sounds of a tattoo machine whirring, "Are you here for Tine?"

The shop is decorated in wood, taxidermy mounts, and airy plants draped from floor to ceiling. It's a scene from a still life painting, and for all the calm exuded by the studio, Tine seems restless, like she'll never be still as long as people can impact her and her art.

She talks about what started as an apartment hunt and ended with finding the perfect space in the exact location she's always wanted for a shop. Over the next year, she built everything from gutting the original space. Her friend Elizabeth from Asrai Garden, a local floral and design store, was ready to help her design the shop. During that time, she tattooed out of other studios with friends like Esther Garcia of Butterfat Studios, who now tattoos at Black Oak.

Tine has been tattooing for the past twelve years. She started an apprenticeship out in Indiana and moved her way through shops in Chicago. She talks about her travels, and how her work wouldn't be where it is today without the people she's met. It's been only about six years since Tine started doing black work, the specialty that's earned her a formidable wait list. She met someone who did the linear, floral black work before it was well known in the United States. "It's all about the experience. It's about the interaction with the people. The tattoo is why they're here, but I've met so many amazing humans through tattooing."

I asked, "Why Black Oak Tattoo?"

"I want to be a sanctuary for all people. Giving people of all walks of life a safe space to get a tattoo. We're in a weird place now and I want people to feel good to be whoever they are. I will do that tattoo and that person will have that for the rest of their life. It's both momentary and really powerful."

PMA Tattoo, Pittsburgh

I t's Sunday morning. Sara Eve Rivera, owner of PMA Tattoo in Pittsburgh, just had her parents over to her studio to help her fix the shop's floor. She's excited to talk because Thursday, October 4, is the one-year anniversary of her shop. She's fought hard for this.

"I've had four or five apprenticeships. Sometimes I was fired for not putting out," she says. She explains that it wasn't till years later when her friends told her to quit being polite to the men who fired her that she knew why.

When Sara worked the front desk at another shop, the artists would be upstairs, and she'd go up to tell them about walk-in clients. One artist would charge up for black clients. Defending him, the manager would argue that darker skin was harder to tattoo.

"It's not harder; it's just different," she explains. Skin is unique to each body: there is no "harder," only different. Nobody is made of paper.

It's hard to hear these stories but easy to understand her desire to create something different. A year ago, Rivera walked out of her job without a plan. The culture at various shops meant regularly defending herself, her clients, and even clients of other artists. She'd try to educate, but more often than seeing change, she'd have to adapt.

The day she announced she was opening her shop was the day the Rock and Roll Hall of Fame announced Bad Brains as an inductee.

"Bad Brains was the first minority punk band I heard. Most of what I heard growing up in State College was 'fuck the government,' but they came from a different perspective. The song 'Attitude' would amp me up. I thought about it in reference to myself."

Sara has social anxiety. She also has PMA ("Positive Mental Attitude") tattooed right below her wrist so as she leans in to someone's body, she can see the letters as a reminder. "You get one shot and you're responsible for every line, but there's no reason to criticize yourself endlessly. Nobody's perfect."

Sara talks of hope. She's seeing more and more women and queer people tattooing. When she started, different types of people weren't visible. It was discouraging. These days she works with other shops and owners like Michelle Joy or Laura Hammel of Gypsy Tattoo Parlor. She talks about helping younger tattoo artists.

"You have to stick together."

Spirited Tattooing Coalition, Philadelphia

Jasmine Morrell, owner of Spirited Tattooing Coalition in Philadelphia, left home when she was seventeen. Her friend was going to Philadelphia for college and wanted to be around friends and live with someone she knew, so Jasmine took up a job in the café of a small Ethiopian restaurant. She chose tattooing after a couple of months reflecting on life direction. "It was a legitimate career path for a lot of artists instead of just going to art school. I decided to train in an apprenticeship as soon as I turned eighteen."

Jasmine found a shop that would train her. She woke up early to work at the café, then ran over to the tattoo shop till it closed, then she'd come home and do it again. After seven months, they said she was ready to take on clients. After ten years and different shops, she felt ready to open her own.

"I'd been through enough mistreatment working around people—I didn't want to be around that kind of energy. And work is such a huge part of your life. I just didn't have what I needed to lead a fully happy life, but I knew I could change it. I felt powerful in that."

Spirited Tattooing Coalition will be three years old in March. After almost fourteen years living in Philadelphia, Jasmine has spent her entire adult life tattooing, and the shop is just a small part of that time. When I ask her about the community in Philadelphia, I can hear her smile over the phone.

"People are really supportive of each other and show up."

Jasmine talks about the political state of the nation and vulnerability. There are fund-raisers and flash benefits to help different groups and organizations. The shop is a collection point for relief efforts in Puerto Rico, with JetBlue flying supplies out of New York City. Her tone shifts.

There is a pause on the phone line. We're both quiet. "Sometimes I feel I'm at a loss over things happening." I nod in agreement with the full weight of a nation feeling powerless.

Jasmine says pensively, "I'm lucky enough to have this space and opportunity to use my business as part of the community as much as possible. It's an intersectional community. It's not there for just one niche or any one group of people." There is a love for her city and the people that surround her, and she can choose the type of energy that blankets her life.

"As long as people like my work, trust me, and want it, I'm happy. I just want to be able to keep tattooing for as long as I can."

Left to right: Kelli Kikcio, Krista Morgenson, Tea Leigh

Welcome Home Studio,
New York City

Tea Leigh and Kelli Kikcio run Welcome Home Studio, a tattoo shop and studio space in New York City. Kelli met Tea over Instagram. They were longtime admirers of each other's art. They met for the first time over coffee and talked about career and life goals. They hadn't planned to become entwined in business and art.

Tea was doing tattoos out of a studio in a shared artist space where Kelli would do guest spots. Kelli reflects, "If I hadn't had that opportunity, we wouldn't be doing what we do today."

Their tattoo shop is unique in that it functions as a shared space for others—be it artists, musicians, activists, and whoever else is put back into the community and needs visibility. In ten years, they hope to open spaces like theirs in other cities.

Tea says of it, "You help someone in need, especially if they're kindred."

They're grateful for the work previous generations of women have done so they have a path. They both speak with the confidence of persistent self-doubt they have to tamp down.

"Maybe I'm not worthy," Tea says. Kelli follows with, "It's really exciting to be a part of this change of culture. But it felt like I didn't deserve it."

There is an importance to their work and the work of others trying to create a positive space for everyone in tattooing. Many of their clients were too intimidated or uncomfortable asking for the work they wanted, even if they knew their own bodies.

Tea starts, "It's important to take away the arrogance of tattooing," and Kelli finishes, "so normal people can get work and not be judged." The openness and acceptance that has been absent from tattooing is inherent in their business ethos.

Tea explains how they share in their clients' stories: "It falls along the line of intimacy we have with clients. They're strangers when they come to us and they're putting one hundred percent of their trust in us and that's why they're willing to share their story with us. It's part of the physical pain. It's easier to talk about painful things. You have to value each client. That's how you run a freaking business."

NO ONE DOES IT ALONE

On unlearning the myth of individual achievement and building community intentionally

by GRACE D. CHIN

A FEW REFLECTIONS ON
COMMUNITY BY GRACE D. CHIN

✓ ALSO A FEMINIST ARTIST ♥

FOR ABOUT 20 YEARS, MY MOTHER WORKED ON A SERIES OF QUILTS PIECED FROM ~~BAD~~ THE LABELS ON OUR FAMILY'S CLOTHING. IT'S AN INCREDIBLE PIECE; EACH OF THE 10 QUILTS DOCUMENTS 2 YEARS IN THE LIVES OF AN IMMIGRANT FAMILY.

ONE OF THE QUILTS

THOUGH WE OFTEN SPEAK OF COMMUNITY IN POSITIVE TERMS, THEY CAN JUST AS EASILY BE TOXIC. IT'S WHAT HAPPENS WHEN COMMUNITIES ARE NOT CREATED INTENTIONALLY AND GROWTH HAPPENS WITHOUT CAREFUL CULTIVATION.

NOT EVEN OUR JEANS WERE SAFE

SOMEONE IS SITTING IN THE SHADE ~~BECAUSE~~ TODAY BECAUSE SOMEONE PLANTED A TREE A LONG TIME AGO.
- WARREN BUFFETT

WHEN I WAS A CHILD, SHE'D STOP STITCHING TO FLIP A QUILT OVER TO SHOW ME ~~HOW~~ HOW THE BACK WAS JUST AS PRETTY AND MORE INTERESTING THAN THE FRONT. THEN SHE'D POINT OUT ALL THE PLACES THE GARMENTS ~~HAD~~ CAME FROM: INDIA, MEXICO, SRI LANKA, THAILAND, SOUTH KOREA, TURKEY, BANGLADESH, ETC.

IN THE CASE OF THE CONNECTIONS CREATED BY A GLOBAL ECONOMY, IT'S DIFFICULT TO RECOGNIZE THAT AS A COMMUNITY WE BELONG TO. NOT KNOWING THE PEOPLE IN ONE'S COMMUNITY LEADS TO DECISION-MAKING THAT BEST BENEFITS ~~THE~~ AN INDIVIDUAL IN THE PRESENT, RATHER THAN THE WHOLE FOR A LONG TIMEFRAME. *

NOT-SEEING (LITERALLY AND FIGURATIVELY)

THIS WAS MY FIRST UNDERSTANDING OF TWO VERY IMPORTANT THINGS:
- EVERYTHING COMES FROM SOMEWHERE/SOMEONE.
- MY FATE IS TANGLED IN THE FATE OF EVERY OTHER HUMAN BEING PRESENT, PAST, AND FUTURE.

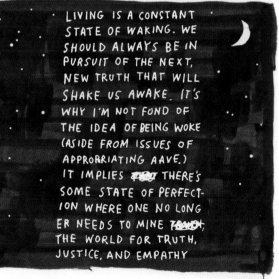

- LIVING IS A CONSTANT STATE OF WAKING. WE SHOULD ALWAYS BE IN PURSUIT OF THE NEXT, NEW TRUTH THAT WILL SHAKE US AWAKE. IT'S WHY I'M NOT FOND OF THE IDEA OF BEING WOKE (ASIDE FROM ISSUES OF APPROPRIATING AAVE.) IT IMPLIES ~~THAT~~ THERE'S SOME STATE OF PERFECTION WHERE ONE NO LONGER NEEDS TO MINE ~~TRUTH~~ THE WORLD FOR TRUTH, JUSTICE, AND EMPATHY

FOR SOME AMOUNT OF TIME (5 MINUTES, A DAY), THE VERY CLOTHES ON MY BACK WERE PART OF ANOTHER PERSON'S LIFE. I'D NEVER MEET THEM, PROBABLY, BUT WE HAD A RELATIONSHIP. IN THIS CASE, IT WAS ■ LIKELY AN EXPLOITIVE ONE. EVEN IF I COULDN'T IMMEDIATELY SEE IT, THE EVIDENCE WAS THERE ONCE I LEARNED TO LOOK. THERE IS EVIDENCE EVERYWHERE OF THESE CONNECTIVE THREADS. SEEKING THEM LEADS TO A CLEARER & RICHER UNDERSTANDING OF OUR WORLD.

STRIVE TO SEE THINGS RELATIONALLY

SEE YOURSELF AS PART OF A
SINGLE WEFT THREAD IN THE
LARGER FABRIC OF HUMAN
HISTORY, A LOOM STRUNG
WITH THE WARP OF TIME.

WE, IN THE PRESENT
DAY ARE ONLY
RESPONSIBLE FOR
WEAVING AS
MUCH AS OUR
SPOOL OF
WEFT WILL
SPAN.

IT IS WORTH MAKING IT AS
BEAUTIFUL AS WE CAN.

IT IS ALSO IMPORTANT TO ACKNOWLEDGE
THAT WE'RE HARVESTING WHAT OUR
PREDECESSORS SOWED (AGAIN, A GOOD
AND A BAD THING). THE NEXT GENER-
ATION WILL DEPEND ON WHATEVER
YIELD WE LEAVE BEHIND. IN SOME WAYS
WE'RE INDEBTED TO THE PEOPLE BEFORE
US. THE BEST WAY TO HONOR THAT IS
TO BROADCAST* SEEDS GENEROUSLY.

IT IS NOT A SPRINT; IT IS NOT EVEN A
MARATHON. IT'S A RELAY. WE'RE A ~~NEW~~
SINGLE RUNNER IN A RACE OF ~~OUR~~
IMMENSE AND INDETERMINATE
DURATION.

  * BROADCAST WAS ORIGINALLY AN
  AGRICULTURAL TERM -- SO COOL!

OUR DUTY IS TO PASS THE BATON IN
GOOD TIME, PERHAPS EVEN TO MAKE UP
DISTANCE OUR PREDECESSORS LOST.
  HOW FAR CAN WE PUSH TOGETHER?

IT'S THIS QUESTION I THINK
A HEALTHY AND INTENTIONAL
COMMUNITY ANSWERS.

AMERICANS IN PARTICULAR ARE NOT FOND
OF NARRATIVES ABOUT COLLECTIVES. ~~DAT~~
THOUGH THE PHRASE "WE THE PEOPLE"
IS THE FOUNDATION OF OUR COUNTRY'S
BIRTH, THE CULT OF ~~HUMAN~~ CELEBRITY
IS SO PERVASIVE THAT WE OFTEN FAIL
TO SEE THE WAYS IN WHICH OUR HEROES/
HEROINES ONLY FOUND SUCCESS BECAUSE
THEY WERE BUTTRESSED BY A COMM-
UNITY OF SUPPORTERS. WE PUT ENTIRELY
TOO MUCH FAITH IN INDIVIDUAL HUMAN
BEINGS, AND SHOULDN'T BE SURPRISED
WHEN THEY LET US DOWN.

NO ONE HAS EVER
DONE ANYTHING
ALONE.

WE ALSO DISLIKE ACCEPTING HELP,
BECAUSE OUR CULTURE FROWNS UPON IT
ON MULTIPLE LEVELS. THE IDEA OF
DEPENDING ON MANY ~~PEOPLE~~ OTHER
PEOPLE IS PERCEIVED AS A DEFICIENCY
OF VIRTUE AND THUS A WELL-DESERVED
FAILURE.

  BUT WAIT THERE'S ⟶
  MORE!

I-LEARNED THE HARD WAY THAT I'D INTERNALIZED SOME OF THESE CULTURAL SCRIPTS ABOUT SELF-SUFFICIENCY.

I'D BEEN STUBBORNLY IGNORING ISSUES WITH MY MENTAL HEALTH. THE LONGER I NEGLECTED TO TAKE CARE OF IT, THE LARGER THE PROBLEM GREW. HYPER-FUNCTIONING BECAME MY ARMOR, THE PROOF I NEEDED TO BELIEVE I WAS FINE ON MY OWN.

I WAS FOOLING NO ONE. EVENTUALLY AND INEVITABLY, I RAN OUT OF GAS TO KEEP UP THE CHARADE.

IT WAS MY COMMUNITY'S SUPPORT THAT KEPT ME ALOFT DURING THAT CHAPTER IN MY LIFE.

THE WAY I SEE IT, MY COMMUNITY INVESTED IN MY WELL-BEING AND SOMEDAY, I'D LIKE TO APPRECIATE THE VALUE OF THAT INVESTMENT TENFOLD.

THIS VIRTUOUS CYCLE IS COMMUNITY AT ITS BEST. WHEN SOMEONE NEEDS CARE, IT IS GIVEN TO THEM, NOT NECESSARILY WITH THE EXPECTATION OF ANY RETURN. BUT BECAUSE ITS MEMBERS WANT PASSIONATELY FOR IT TO SUCCEED LONG AFTER THEIR INVOLVEMENT, THEY GIVE BACK.

LEARNING TO STOP SEEING INDIVIDUAL ACHIEVEMENT IN ISOLATION.

IN 2010, I ATTENDED AN ARTIST TALK THAT CHANGED THE WAY I THOUGHT ABOUT ART-MAKING. IT WAS BY ACTIVIST, STREET ARTIST, AND PRINTMAKER SWOON - DELIVERED AS THE OCCUPY WALL STREET ORGANIZING WAS BEGINNING TO COOK, SO IT WAS PUNCTUATED BY SOME SENSE OF URGENCY. WHAT I REMEMBER MOST IS HER PERSISTENT ADVICE TO

FIND YOUR PEOPLE.

THOSE WERE NOT EMPTY WORDS. MUCH OF HER WORK IS COLLABORATIVE AND SHE WAS INTENTIONAL IN NAMING AND CREDITING THOSE COLLABORATORS.

SO COMES THE QUESTION: HOW DOES ONE BUILD COMMUNITY INTENTIONALLY AND EFFECTIVELY?

THE WORLD IS TOO MUCH TO SWALLOW.

THAT SLOGAN "THINK GLOBALLY, ACT LOCALLY" APPLIES HERE.

BREAK IT DOWN INTO MANAGEABLE BITES. START WITH SELF:

WHERE DO YOU STAND IN RELATION TO THE WORLD? PLOT OUT YOUR COORDINATES (IE. AGE, RACE, ~~RACE~~ ETC) WHERE WOULD YOU LIKE TO GO? WHAT CAN YOU OFFER TO OTHER PEOPLE?

NEXT COMES THE PART I FIND MOST CHALLENGING: REACH OUT.

REACHING OUT MEANS LOWERING OUR DEFENSES, WHICH FEELS FRIGHTENING. IT MEANS ACCEPTING THE PROSPECT OF BEING REJECTED.

THEY'LL HATE ME

I'M TOO MESSY

IT'S EASIER NOT TO DO IT.

FOR ME, IT'S THAT I GET CAUGHT UP IN MY OWN VULNERABILITIES AND INSECURITIES THAT I FORGET OTHER PEOPLE MIGHT FEEL THOSE TOO. IT MEANS ALWAYS ASSUMING THAT OTHERS ARE WISER, MORE IN CONTROL, LESS AFRAID OR LESS LONELY THAN YOU.

THAT MIGHT BE TRUE SOME OF THE TIME.

BUT IT'S A PRETTY SELF-CENTERED WAY TO SEE THE WORLD.

THE PEOPLE AROUND YOU HAVE FELT HURT EMBARRASSED, RECKLESS, HEARTBROKEN, OR LONELY. YOU MAY HAVE SOMETHING THAT WILL HELP THEM.

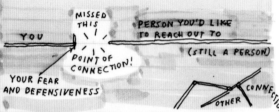

WHEN YOU OPERATE ON THE ASSUMPTION EVERYONE IS BETTER THAN YOU AND WILL NOT BE RECEPTIVE TO YOU, YOUR WORLD BECOMES NARROWER, IN THE WORST WAY.

BEYOND THAT ~~MILD~~ BARRIER OF FEAR, THE REWARD MIGHT BE FAR GREATER THAN THE RISK OF BEING REJECTED BY ONE OF ABOUT 8 BILLION PEOPLE IN THE WORLD.

SO REACH OUT! BE GENUINE (DO NOT ASK FOR LABOR ON THEIR PART FROM THE GET GO).

ONCE YOU'VE BUILT TRUST WITH THE FOLKS YOU'VE REACHED OUT TO, FIND A LARGER PROBLEM TO SOLVE.

WHEN YOU ASKED YOURSELF WHERE YOU WANT TO GO, IS IT SOMEWHERE YOU CAN GO TOGETHER? WITH YOUR COMMUNITY'S SUPPORT, HOW MUCH CHANGE CAN YOU MAKE WITH THE TIME YOU HAVE?

~~YOU~~ KNOWING TO ASK THESE QUESTIONS IS WHAT MAKES AN INTENTIONAL COMMUNITY.

YOU CANNOT CHANGE ANY SOCIETY UNLESS YOU TAKE RESPONSIBILITY FOR IT; UNLESS YOU SEE YOURSELF AS BELONGING TO IT & RESPONSIBLE FOR CHANGING IT.
- GRACE LEE BOGGS

I KNOW I'M NOT ALONE IN FEELING THE WORLD IS A FRIGHTENING PLACE RIGHT NOW. HOWEVER, I TRULY BELIEVE NO ONE SHOULD BEAR THAT WEIGHT ALONE. WITH OTHERS IT BECOMES POSSIBLE TO NOT ONLY CARRY IT, BUT ALSO TO SLOUGH IT OFF.

TOMORROW
BELONGS TO THOSE
OF US WHO CONCEIVE OF
IT AS BELONGING TO
EVERYONE;
WHO LEND THE BEST
OF OURSELVES TO IT
AND WITH JOY.
— Audre Lorde

AGAINST THE GRAIN

by Julia Turshen

photographs by Charlotte O'Donnell

The first substantial thing I built out of wood was a chair that was too big for me, a chair sized for an adult. I made it when I was about seven. My father still has it in his home office. It's a really simple construction—almost Donald Judd–esque. I made it at school, where there was supervision and help, but still, at seven, I made something useful that's lasted for decades.

The school in question was a free-spirited one where we called our teachers by their first names. It was an empowering place to be a young person, especially a young girl, since the playing field was so level. It was a place where it was okay to not excel at something the first time, if at all. My favorite class was woodshop because not only did I get to cut wood with saws, hammer it with nails, and make things that had function: I also got to feel invincible. I learned that I could make things with my own two hands that served a purpose.

Julia Turshen, Age 4

In a way, it's exactly what I do now as a cookbook author who spends most of my time working on recipes in my kitchen. Cooking and woodworking actually have quite a lot in common. They both require specific tools (some of these even overlap: the popular Microplane grater originated as a woodworking tool) to make something practical with your hands. They both require some type of ingredient, whether it be maple syrup or a piece of maple, that gets combined with something else or just spruced up and presented in its own glory. They both involve constant problem-solving, and both allow you to learn something new every day. And both are male-dominated fields that tend to use all of the gear, skills, and vocabulary as a sort of invisible wall of intimidation to keep the boys safely in their clubs.

Enter Sarah Marriage, a classically trained furniture maker who saw the gender barriers and discrimination in her field and did what she does best: she built something beautiful with intention and purpose. A Workshop of Our Own (referred to as "WOO") is her professional woodworking space built by and for women and gender-nonconforming craftspeople and community members. Located in Baltimore, it's in a large building that's easy to spot since a colorful mural covers its brick walls.

While I didn't make woodworking my career, it continues to be my hobby and I have always valued the exposure I had to it at such a young age in such a particular space. I am so glad Sarah has created a similar atmosphere at WOO and that everyone who visits and works there can be part of a collective that's as supportive as it is empowering.

I got to talk to Sarah recently about her road to WOO, her goals and dreams, and her thoughts about power tools and hardware stores. I am so inspired by her creation and her vision. What follows is an edited version of our conversation.

If you had to sum up WOO in a sentence, what would you say?

I usually say it's a 6,400-square-foot professionally equipped educational workshop for women and gender-nonconforming folks.

What kinds of spaces were you working in before WOO?

I had worked in a shared workshop where one guy had a lease and had had it for decades, and there were three or four other people who worked at the shop at the same time and paid rent to him. We shared large machines and everyone had their own hand tools. I've also spent time in academic environments (I went to woodworking school at the College of the Redwoods and was a fellow at the Center for Furniture Craftsmanship).

When exactly did you open WOO?

We were officially open for business in late April 2017. I got the lease in September 2016. We worked on the building for a long time. We got electrical in March and we opened in April. We had just one electric panel that worked . . . the rest were busted.

You keep saying "we." Who is the "we"?

It is me. The "we" should be an "I." But it is "we" in the sense of living out loud and putting my work on social media, and having a lot of support from people right away and having people being interested in being a part of it. I've also sort of thought about the project as belonging to everybody. And I had a lot of volunteers. From about October of last year we started having volunteer weekends. In January I hired a helper and she was supposed to work for me for about three weeks, but it ended up being about six months. We now have an advisory board, so there are four other women I meet with once a month to talk about the mission and how everything is going. They also do a fair amount of volunteer work. They're members. One is a furniture maker, one is an architect, another is a local public

school teacher, and the fourth is a metalworker who runs another maker space in town.

How did you find the building?

It was kind of luck. I came down to Baltimore to start the project and was looking for a commercial space. I found a realtor and it just so happened it was the first place we went. It had just been purchased by a real estate investor. It had gone on the rental market for the first time in years and years. I really liked the windows and the size and that it was a fixer-upper (which matched our budget).

Once you found the space, how did you pay for it?

The project was pretty much built with a grant through the Society of Arts and Crafts through the John D. Mineck Furniture Fellowship, personal assistance from family, and a few future commissioned promises.

And what happens in that space?

One of the core principles is what we call "professionals in residence." So there's space for four women or nonbinary makers to run their business out of the space and be the backdrop for everything that goes on here. This gives students and apprentices the opportunity to see women and gender-nonconforming makers making a living doing this work. The emphasis of the project is amplifying voices of underrepresented members in our field and changing the perception of what it means to be a woodworker.

What's the feeling when you walk in the door?

It's a massive, cavernous space. It's almost cathedral-like. It's a long, narrow building with 24-foot ceilings with quite a lot of height. It feels perhaps even larger than it actually is because of that headroom. When you enter, you walk through the machine room, so you have to put on protective equipment if there's work going on. That's where all the loud, noisy work happens. There's a break with a wall with two giant double doors and that opens to the bench room, where all the handwork happens . . . gluing, etc.

Sarah Marriage

The emphasis of the project is amplifying voices of underrepresented members in our field and changing the perception of what it means to be a woodworker.

Was that setup intentional or just how it fell into place?
It's kind of just how it fell into place. Mostly because the first room doesn't have any windows, but the second room has about forty. I wanted the bench room to be the one that had all of the natural light.

How did you decide on the name?
It's a nod to Virginia Woolf and her essay "A Room of One's Own," and it kind of happened spontaneously when I was first talking about the project and wasn't sure where I was going to end up. I was trying to explain the idea to my uncle and I was saying "It's just a woodshop that's all women working together," and he was like "I don't get it," and I said "It's a workshop of our own," and he's a very literary guy so the idea worked.

Your logo is pretty genius.
It was inspired by the poster Sheila Levrant de Bretteville designed in 1974 for an event at the Los Angeles–based Woman's Building titled "Women in design: the next decade: a conference for women who work with public visual and physical forms." When WOO started to become a reality, I looked up Sheila and wrote her an email. I went up to Yale to talk to her and she said, "Sure, you can use it." We styled it a bit differently than she did.

That's awesome that you went and asked her in person.
I think it was important to do. I like the idea that we're connected to this progression of history.

Has your work changed at all with your surroundings?
I haven't been able to do a lot of my own work lately, but the things I have been designing have changed. I don't know entirely what to attribute it to. I think, if anything, Baltimore has changed my work a lot. Just thinking about sustainability and reuse and affordability.

Was that not a priority to you before?
At the end of the day, a lot of the furniture that I've made has been extremely expensive. I'm now thinking more about ways of producing furniture that reduce the cost of it and considering the materials that already exist in the world.

And that has to do with Baltimore?
I think so. Reclaimed materials are a huge part of the work that is going on around me here. Even more so is that the students coming here say they want to have nice things, but nice things cost a lot. So I'm thinking of projects that students can make that are really nice but don't cost a lot. It's hard because woodworking is a really expensive hobby (and an expensive profession). Not just the tooling, but also the materials themselves. The workshop helps cut down on the tooling costs. But furniture-grade material costs a lot, so using things that already exist makes a lot of sense.

You offer a lot of classes. Who comes to them?
We get a lot of artists and we have a pretty good range of ages. There are young people in their early twenties who are still figuring out what they want to do and are interested in learning woodworking for reasons like building skills or wanting to get a job in it or who have always wanted to but never had an opportunity to learn. And there are women who come in specifically because they say they have never felt comfortable taking a class somewhere else. We get people who are professionals in other fields and are looking for something creative to do in their nonworking time. We get a lot of people who are homeowners who want to work on their places and want to learn how to use tools. And we get a lot of older, retired women who want to make furniture or household items either for themselves or to launch a small business or to influence their artistic practice.

And who do you wish you saw more often in your classes?
We get a lot of interest from parents in having classes for children and we want to do that, so that's coming along on the horizon. I taught a class for four kids last night; it was really fun.

What did you teach them?
I taught them how to use a band saw and how to carve using gauges. Three made swords and one cut out the shape of a flame on a piece of maple. She thought she saw the figure of a flame, so she made a little sculpture.

You do youth outreach and offer internships. How did these programs come about and what purpose do they serve?
Anything we do with youth outreach has a couple of purposes. The way in which it's related to our mission is to

normalize women as leaders in this field. So when girls and boys are taught how to do woodworking by women, that's a powerful, fundamental experience seeing women doing this work. As far as for kids in general, I think woodworking is an incredibly awesome thing for their brains, up there with playing an instrument. It's a different way to engage your mind and body. It's math without numbers. It's also kind of like a sport because you're building muscle memory. The internship program, which we hope will become a more intense apprenticeship program, is currently a three-to-six-month program where you get trained in machine maintenance and woodworking. The hope is to turn it into small production furniture and product making. My goal is to have members come together and work together to design some products, a line of furniture specifically, that apprentices could make and learn small batch production skills, and the sale of that work would fund the apprenticeship program and help the overhead of the woodshop.

Do you have any dreams for WOO?
Oh, sure, so many! I'd really love to have a residency, whether it's once a year or something so that we're able to attract a woman in the field who is an expert woodworker who could spend time working here and be around the students and the members. We're hoping to have some kind of women in furniture making summit to talk about women in the field.

If you could fast-forward a decade, where do you see WOO?
In ten years I hope that we have trained enough people that we have an awesome workforce of women furniture makers and woodworkers here teaching other women and moderating community shop hours so the place is living and breathing on its own. I hope the environment continues to be a space where you're not a woman woodworker, you're just a woodworker. And you can come in and have a wonderful, creative environment around you where you can bounce ideas around. And we're building up longer form classes. We're hoping to have some weeklong workshops in the summer.

What would you say to someone who is afraid to pick up a power tool?
It's okay to be afraid. Fear's not a bad thing. But let's talk

about what this machine does and how the physics of it work, where the forces are, and what could happen with it. Let's reduce fear through understanding the tool and how it works and that you're the one controlling it.

Does that always work?
If a student is still afraid, I work with them to use it. I've had a few students who are shaking when they're halfway through a table saw cut. I turn off the machine and we go for a walk or do a few jumping jacks. And usually after a few cuts, the fear is gone. But if I wasn't there in person, I would say it's okay to be afraid and it's not going to hurt you if you learn how it works. Know it's going to be noisy.

And what would you say to that same person if they feel intimidated when they walk into a hardware store?
I'd say what someone told me the first time I gave a lecture: "You know what you're going to say and you know that you're right." Don't take any crap from anybody. Which is easier said than done.

And how do you feel when you walk into a hardware store?
I feel like people are looking at me and don't expect that I'm a professional. That's okay because I am one and I am going to get the stuff that I need, and if I need help, I'll ask for it, and if I don't, then leave me alone. I was blocked from entering a lumberyard once. In those cases I get really serious and just hold my own.

Right on. Anything else you might want to add?
I appreciate that you didn't ask me any questions about men. That's what everyone else asks.

What about men?
Like how do men feel about the project and can they be part of it?

Oh, well, I'm not that interested in that.
Ha! Well, one thing I might add is that women have been making furniture for millennia. In recent history, it's been uncommon for women to do this work, but it's increasingly common. And I think we're at a point now where there's enough of us doing this professionally that instead of just being tough and making furniture alone, there's enough of us to get together and support each other.

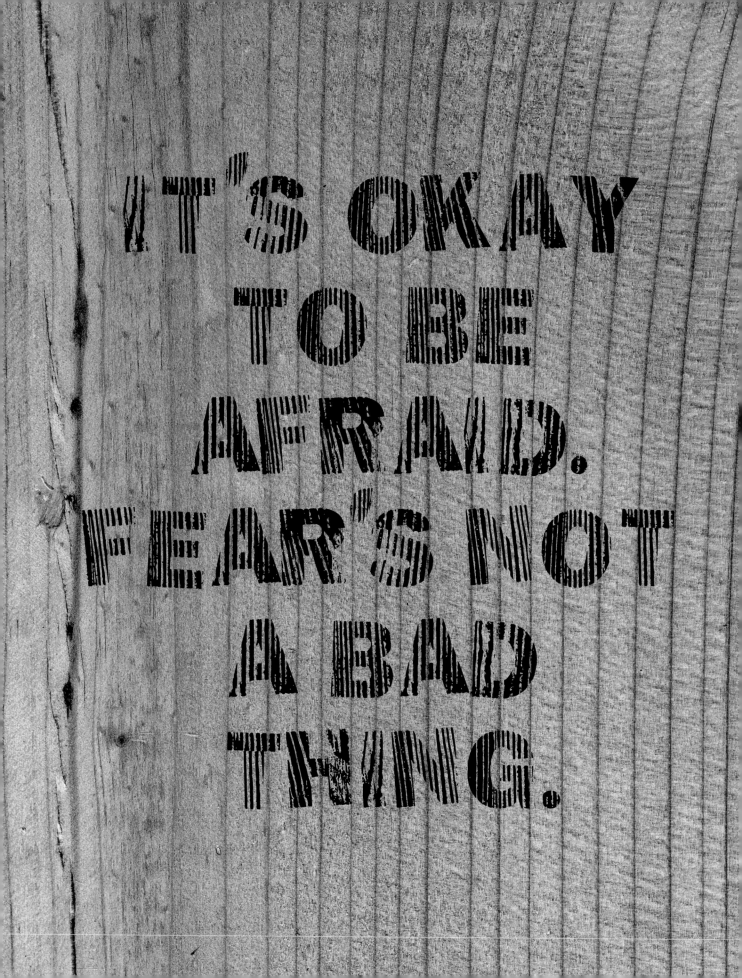

COMMUNITY HEROES

Nina F. Ichikawa
Writer and Policy Director at
Berkeley Food Institute

My grandmother graduated from
UC Berkeley in 1939 with a degree
in nutrition. At that time, many
universities would not enroll Asian
Americans. She was dedicated to
learning about and spreading the
word about the health benefits of
Japanese food.

Elsie Adachi Ogata

After *T Magazine*'s tribute to Michelle Obama, her profile image became
my iPhone screensaver. It's a conversation starter. "Is that the First Lady
on your phone? Do you know her?" It's a frequent reminder that inspira-
tional people need a special place, the same reverence as R&B posters
that hung on my adolescent bedroom wall. I watch their movements—
healers, writers, gardeners, and entrepreneurs gliding in their fields and
lighting paths.

Just like a vase holding baseball bat–size gladiolus, many vibrant
women lift me. I romanticized power lunches with my industry movers
and shakers. My idea of the ultimate mentor has evolved. I've tossed out
the one person notion and lean in to the idea that coaches are in constant
rotation. Moments of awakening and motivation have come from my community, extraordinary individuals making quiet home runs.

I reached out to ten women to see who their inspirations and
mentors were.

_____

by Nicole A. Taylor

Gabrielle Fulton Ponder
Playwright and
Independent Filmmaker

Toni Morrison, who in addition to being a Nobel Prize– and Pulitzer Prize–winning novelist is a playwright. The dialogue in Ms. Morrison's novels ripples with theatricality. I am a huge fan because of her attention to detail and love for the subject matter that emanates from the page.

Kendra Feather
Restaurateur

My friend AnnMarie owns a cycling studio here in Richmond, Virginia. It's only now—in my mid-forties—that I feel like I've found a peer whom I can talk business with. Working through things like social media or looking for new locations, our "co-mentoring" gives me a fresh look.

Gabrielle Etienne
Culinary Creative

She lives on Sapelo Island, Georgia, and is my inspiration to move into this conscious space of cooking for greater substance than just sustenance. Mrs. Cornelia managed to do this unknowingly, with her writings about her ancestral knowledge, strong acceptance, and pride taken in her inheritance.

Toni Morrison

AnnMarie Grohs

Cornelia Bailey

Sarah Keough
Photographer and Editor

The person I'm writing about is Jessica Craig-Martin, a photographer. I liked her work personality—smart, irreverent, strange—even before I showed up to her class. She was critical of the rich society people she was photographing, but she did it with heart and a kind of maniacal joy.

Lesley Ware
Author and Fashion Expert

Kimberly's interviews with authors, yogis, entrepreneurs, and artists helped me envision my own creative life. At the time I was working a full-time job and feeling stuck. After attending Kimberly's weekend-long yoga and creativity retreats, I started to see my potential as a creative and began to infuse tranquility and creative visioning into my days.

Leni Sorensén, PhD
Food Historian

Karen is my living example of Christianity at its best. As an unbeliever, I am always warmed by her generous spirit of nonjudgment. She has a fighting spirit that was tried in a long battle within the NAACP community over the presidency of that organization. She lost that particular contest, but the battle itself roused the group to a new level of awareness.

Jessica Craig-Martin

Kimberly Wilson

Karen Waters-Wicks

Aki Baker
Co-founder of MINKA Brooklyn

Adaku is the embodiment of a graceful warrior, whose mission is anchored in the love for her people, and her work continues to support the transformation of young people in many ways. The words that come to me when I think of Adaku are "elegant fierceness."

Anu Prestonia
Artist and Entrepreneur

Oprah has inspired countless others and instead of resting on her laurels and remaining comfortable, she stretched herself to leave her celebrated throne as talk-show host. She created a network to inspire people to look within to heal themselves. It is also my mission to communicate, inspire, and help others through spiritual awareness to acknowledge, address, and heal themselves, seeking the highest form of beauty inside and out.

Stacia Brown
Writer and Audio Producer

Tomika Anderson is the mother of a young son, a veteran magazine journalist, the founder of *Single Parents Who Travel,* and a co-founder of *Motivated Mamas.* She has single-handedly coordinated group parent-and-child outings for dozens of families to everywhere from Broadway shows to Caribbean cruise destinations.

Adaku Utah

Oprah Winfrey

Tomika Anderson

The Power of Place

Sometimes a place can make a person. The place that made me was the cragged, rocky, sea-sprayed coast of Maine.

by Megan Wood

photographs by Greta Rybus

I was fortunate enough to grow up there, on a small island at the edge of the earth, home to rugged, salt-cured fishermen and descendants of Italian immigrant quarrymen. It was a place I fled as soon as possible, to "see the world," but it was the place, too, that always called me back. Pulled by tides and seasons, I finally surrendered to my home. Moving back to such a rural place was frustrating for the same reasons it was attractive—isolation and simplicity. But I found that this place has a way of finding and feeding the strength we diminish inside ourselves.

When I moved home, I did any and all odd jobs. I worked as a line cook, a bartender, a sternman, and a housepainter before I realized that to really find your place here, you have to make it yourself. Shortly after that realization I met the woman who would become my business partner and we schemed up an idea that would become a successful business, growing and dynamic with year-round employees and two properties. In making space and creating a life in this rugged place, I found beacons of strength in visionary women who had done before me what I felt in my bones I wanted to do, who had left other worlds or moved home to re-create a truth that lives so strongly in this place of Maine.

Ingrid was a pioneer and a lightning rod. To say Maine's working waterfront is male dominated is an understatement. The self-described cowboys of the ocean pride themselves on working extreme hours in extreme weather for extreme profit. Historically, the role of women has been one of support, and it has been largely homebound. This binary saturates the culture of fishing. Men pass on unwritten knowledge of the seafloor, fish and bird migrations, hidden ledges, and seasonal weather patterns to their sons and crack crude jokes to each other over the CB radio. Women make the homes, raise the children, prepare the lunches, and wash bait-soaked clothes. The community that Ingrid called home—Stonington, Maine—embodied the quintessential working waterfront. She was a native New Yorker and had spent extensive time traveling and living around the world—including in Mexico, Nicaragua, Greece, France, Israel, and Russia. She is proficient in Russian and French. She authored several acclaimed short essays and books, and at the young age of twenty-eight gained recognition and was nominated for a National Book Award for her book *Combat in the Erogenous Zone* (Knopf, 1972). This book and other essays brought her fame, but this spotlight and urban bustle was not the life she wanted. With her earnings from published writing, she bought a house and moved to Maine. She chose Stonington as her home and made the fisheries her business.

Ingrid created Ingrid Bengis Seafood (est. 1985) as a direct connection between top chefs from across the country and fishermen, crab pickers, urchin divers, and oyster farmers long before "farm to table" eateries were a trending obsession. She believed Stonington and its fisheries offered something unique that should be recognized and valued. Ingrid was seen by many as a fierce predator on the docks. To others she was fearless, driven, and a perfectionist. She was shrewd and demanded the freshest and highest quality catch from fishermen, harvesters, and farmers. Her demeanor and presence was one of passion and conviction; she would talk over, walk out on, and dismiss people or conversations that she saw as irrelevant to

INGRID BENGIS

her motive. She built a reputation for superb quality that was sought after by chefs, and she insisted they come and visit her in Stonington, so they could see where the scallops, lobster, and crab were being harvested and meet the fishermen and their families who worked, sometimes risking their lives, to harvest these products. Ingrid was adamant that the fishermen and chefs knew each other, understood that they were in the pursuit of quality and value together. She saw and filled the need for a seafood monger who could both negotiate prices on the dock and guarantee quality to the chef. Ingrid built her business from the shore up, and she established herself as an unflinching advocate for the fishermen and farmers of Stonington. She met the clammers at dawn, the crab pickers at noon, the lobster boats in the afternoon, and the FedEx pickup on time. She provided the freshest and highest quality products, and the chefs she worked with staked their reputations on it.

To see a woman on the docks was a rarity, but Ingrid made her presence known. She created a market that was not previously there, and she required and delivered the best. She understood the marketability of a place in the form of a product procured directly from the fishermen. One of her trademarks was the peekytoe crab, a native pest to the lobster trap that she rebranded as a delicacy. She thrived on the ego of the fishing industry and embraced the rugged culture as part of her. The passion and drive she brought to Ingrid Bengis Seafood and Stonington has assured a place for Maine seafood on the most acclaimed menus and in the most elite kitchens.

Ingrid passed away in the summer of 2017 after years of fighting cancer. She left behind a family, a thriving business, and an absence that cannot be filled. I was fortunate enough to share an island home with Ingrid and a summer birthday. We made a point to find each other in the heat and hustle of summer to sit outside with a glass of wine and talk about the particular struggles of business and small-town living. She was relentless in her support of any female entrepreneur and in her vision to create a connection between place and people in this unique community.

To visit The Lost Kitchen is to feel at home: all the comforts of family, loved possessions, and food prepared with exquisite passion. This is the intention and the creation of Erin French. Rendered from the remains of a historic mill and perched over a harnessed stream, her restaurant embodies what it means to make our home and heart our work. Erin has meticulously created every detail of this restaurant. As the name suggests, The Lost Kitchen has had multiple reincarnations, starting as a pop-up dinner club in her home to a mobile custom-designed Airstream to its final home in the historic Mill among the rolling hills of Freedom, Maine. Erin grew up here, a place that seems midway between anywhere—a few hours north of Augusta, south of Bangor, and inland from the coast. She has carved out a life where there was nothing before, only a place that called her home.

Today The Lost Kitchen is one of the most sought-after dining experiences in Maine. The phone line opens up at midnight on a day in April and all reservations for the year are filled before the day is out. This is the demand she has created, on her terms, from her vision and from her heart. The menu is never the same, never repeating, never without the most current and

ERIN FRENCH

freshest seasonal ingredients. She welcomes guests into her restaurant as if she were welcoming home old friends. The ruralness and destination quality of The Lost Kitchen add to its magical allure. It is thrilling to travel so off the beaten path and to find a restaurant of such simple perfection. it has been nominated several times for a James Beard Award. Erin has been propositioned by critics and investors to build bigger, build more, expand the space, open earlier, stay open later in the season, etc., but she has always declined. That is not the model she intended. She has recently published her first cookbook, which serves as a portal inviting the reader in to the beautifully curated life Erin has created for herself.

When I first met Erin and started working with her, it was her clarity and drive that were undeniably attractive. She is unwavering in knowing what she wants. Her commitment to perfection comes across in every part of The Lost Kitchen. Her determination to create a place where there was none and to know what will work,

what is real, what is right, and what feels like home comes down to how Erin has embraced the place where she is from and answered the call to grow, nurture, and thrive where she was planted.

Sometimes the journey is the adventure, people say, and if North Haven and Cecily Pingree's Calderwood Hall is your destination, you had better enjoy the journey, because it is a ways from anywhere. The island is part of the Penobscot Bay archipelago, one of many islands including my own, but unlike in Deer Isle, there is no bridge. The ferry departs the small fishing town three times a day in the winter as the population shrinks to a quarter of what it is in the summer. The hour-long ride gives time for contemplation and adjustment before entering this slow, small town.

CECILY PINGREE

Cecily grew up on North Haven, where you know everyone and everyone knows you. In a town so closely knit in the winter, it can be a jarring adjustment in the spring when ferry load after ferry load of "people from away" arrive in North Haven. This influx of outsiders boosts the economy and makes many people's year-round incomes possible; however, it is not without social chafing. Uniting two distinct parts of the community—the visitor, vacationer, and second (or third) homeowner with the working fisherman, the carpenter, and the farmer—is no easy feat, but that is exactly what Cecily has done with her creation of Calderwood Hall market and restaurant.

The large classic New England Mansard building sits just a few hundred yards from the ferry terminal and the commercial piers where most fishermen keep their boats and sell their daily catch of lobsters. Cecily bought the building that had been the central meeting place of the island community over its hundred-year history, a place for dances, basketball games, and town meetings. Her vision was to create a year-round restaurant, market, and brewery with on-site housing. In a time when more and more young people were leaving the island to find jobs and community elsewhere, Cecily took on the project to create a space that would support a community identity.

To enter the renovated community hall on any summer evening is to be met with a cacophony of celebrations: bellowing fishermen, deaf from the long day aboard their diesel-engine boats, screaming children, clanging pots from the open kitchen, and laughter ringing through the room. The setting is informal: long community tables obligate strangers to sit next to each other, to engage in conversation. The menu is simple and perfect: there is a rotating variety of pizzas topped with fresh ingredients from the island's farms. Summer favorites include peach and prosciutto, or goat cheese and fig. The salads are made from local greens and topped with ingredients picked from the farm that day. The food is fresh and the facilities a new rendering of the historic rural community. Cecily's clarity in her intention to create a welcoming space is impressive. The space comes alive, as a beacon to newcomers, old friends, even some enemies. The hall incites engagement and creates community.

Maine is rugged, it is remote, it can be isolating in the extreme, but it is also in these small towns and on these remote islands that the spark of community thrives in people. To choose to leave urban comforts and make something where there was nothing before is terrifying, but it is also exhilarating. These small rural communities can be the most fertile for unique business opportunities to take root and thrive in. Towns built on strong work ethics and the tight-knit fabric of chosen family create the structure and support that is unique and undeniably powerful, where all you have to do is breathe life into a dream and create a home for it among the rocky cliffs, deep in the quiet forest, in the dark frozenness of winter, and under the star-strewn sky. What these three exceptional women have taught me and continue to remind me is that if you allow it and if you listen to it, a place can be a powerful partner.

Left to right: Amilia Campbell, Cecily Pingree, Lydia Brown, Jessica Hallowell

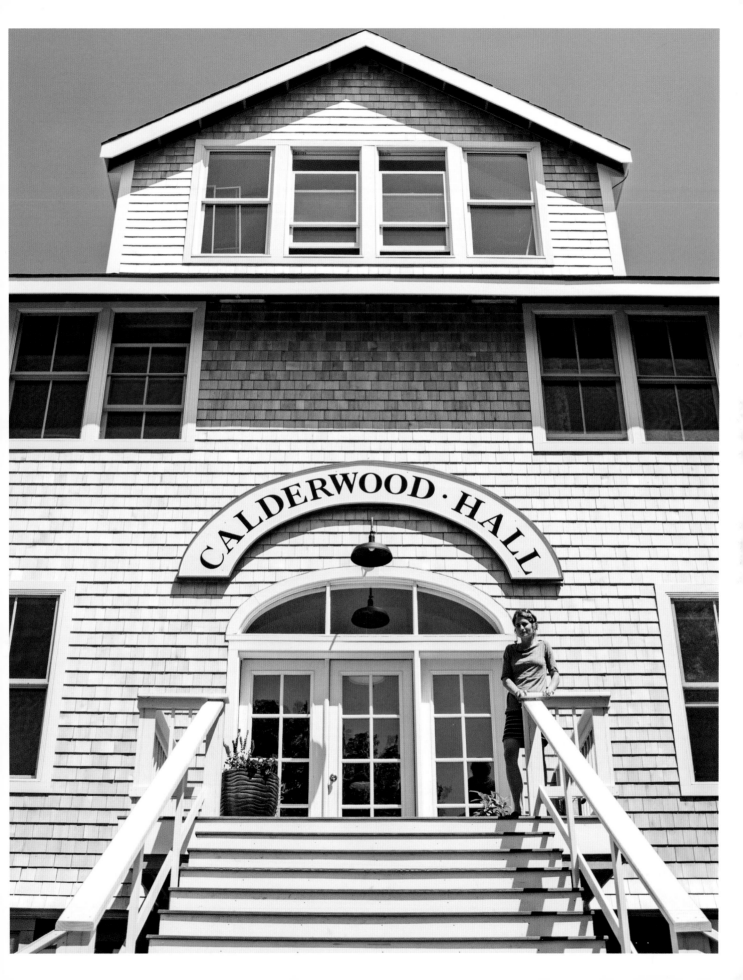

In making space and creating a life in this rugged place, I found beacons of strength in visionary women who had done before me what I felt in my bones I wanted to do.

—Megan Wood

How have you used your
platform and voice
(online and off) to effect
change in your community?

by Grace Bonney
illustrations by Avery Kua

The only constant in life is change, but what happens when progress doesn't come fast enough? I spoke with four powerful creatives—chef Preeti Mistry of Juhu Beach Club and Navi Kitchen; writer and Black Contemporary Art founder Kimberly Drew; host of WNYC's "Death, Sex and Money," Anna Sale; and fashion designer Bethany Yellowtail of B. Yellowtail—about the changes they'd like to see in their communities and what they're doing to inspire that growth.

PREETI: I have always used whatever platform that comes to me to effect change in our restaurant community and to educate people on the realities of our industry. I'm honest with journalists about how I feel. Leading by example is the best way. I think our restaurants engage the community by donating to organizations that are important to us, like Black Lives Matter, Destiny Arts Center, Standing Rock Sioux Tribe, and UndocuFund. Recently I have been involved with doing dinners that bring community members together, and I plan to do more of these. I think it is a great way to engage people in a particular cause or community, when you break bread together.

ANNA: I think a lot of us in the United States (and really, across the English-speaking world) are trying to make sense of how digital connectivity can feed us rather than just separate and isolate us. Through direct conversations about taboo areas of life with a surprising and varied mix of guests, including our listeners, we've really tried to be an antidote to that. We focus on big moments of transition but also mundane details of what our lives look like these days. Yes, people most often listen alone to podcasts, but my hope is that after an episode, our listeners exhale, lift their eyes, and feel a deeper sense of connection with the people physically around them.

BETHANY: There is natural artistic and entrepreneurial instinct in my community. It comes from resilience and an inherent nature to make beautiful things out of limited resources, just like our ancestors have always done. I recognize this and have used my platform and voice to activate like-minded Native folks so that we can share our own stories and messages using art and fashion as a catalyst. Although the mainstream fashion industry has never authentically included the first designers of this nation, we're carving out our own space so that we can be the change our communities need.

KIMBERLY: For the past seven years, I've fashioned a career out of screaming into the internet about the things that need to change in the world. Offline, I have tough conversations, show up for folks, and try my damnedest to walk my talk online.

Q

What are some of the biggest issues/ challenges within your community that you would like to see change?

PREETI: The restaurant industry is still dominated by white men. They get the media attention, endorsements, TV shows, and investors. My hope is that we as an industry realize how toxic the culture is and learn to change from it. That means not just creating safe work environments, but also seeing more women and people of color being given more attention in the media, opportunities to grow and be promoted, access to capital to build their dream restaurants, etc.

BETHANY: One of the largest challenges that Native American communities face is that our people and our issues are not included, recognized, or humanized in the mainstream or general public consciousness. It's difficult to create change for our communities when the narratives about our people are primarily created and advanced by non-Natives. New narratives created by Native peoples are necessary and desperately needed.

KIMBERLY: I am sick and tired of plastic bags. I really hope that in the coming years, New York City will think about ways to encourage its citizens to get greener. As a city, we really abuse single-use plastics.

Q

What person or project that you admire has made a real change or difference within your community?

PREETI: La Cocina, a kitchen incubator supporting women of color entrepreneurs in the hospitality industry, is one that has had so many amazing WOC chefs who have gone on to have their own successful businesses. It's a real inspiration to see all the amazing women that have come out of that kitchen to open their own independent restaurants and businesses.

ANNA: I am always studying people who seem to have taken a robust digital presence and transformed it into real change and relationships on the ground, and I don't think anyone has done that better than writer Ashley Ford. I've been so inspired by the way she lifts up others by being open and curious and uncertain in public and is always finding ways to direct those relationships to action.

KIMBERLY: I absolutely love Carri Twigg. She is my go-to for an update on global politics. She was working in Obama's White House in her twenties. She's been changing the world as we know it since she was like eight years old.

BETHANY: Thosh Collins and Chelsey Luger, founders of Well for Culture (an indigenous health initiative), have helped many of us, including me, visualize what indigenous well-being looks like. Through stories, photographs, videos, and songs, they teach and promote healthy lifestyles, re-indigenized diets, indigenized fitness methods, and mental/spiritual connectedness. Strong tribal nations are built by strong individuals, so seeing them encourage wellness as a way to sustain, rebuild, and strengthen our communities is inspiring.

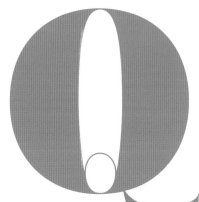

How do you stay motivated or reinspire yourself when changes are difficult or slow to happen?

PREETI: I think it's important to always remember that old phrase "No one can do everything, but everyone can do something."

ANNA: I turn back to the work and get into the studio and do an interview. That connects me back to the energizing challenge of our mission: to amplify the multiple dimensions of our humanity with humor, honesty, humility . . . and uncomfortable questions.

KIMBERLY: I have some of the world's most amazing friends. They are my everything. I count my nuclear family in that category as well. I love that my parents are my friends, too.

BETHANY: I reconnect. Most of the work I do happens out of my office in Los Angeles, which is far from my home on the Crow and Northern Cheyenne nations. I go home to remind myself about what is truth, what is real, and what is necessary. It always fuels the fire inside me to keep going.

What advice do you have for people who would like to get involved and make a real change within their own community?

PREETI: Talk to folks who are already doing things in your community and see how you can help. Especially if you are white, male, and/or cisgender, make sure you don't fall into the "savior syndrome." Center yourself in your quest to effect change. We have a long history of folks who have been fighting the good fight for decades. Honor them and learn from them.

ANNA: Notice when you are feeling adrift and disconnected, and pay attention to when that feeling lifts. Do more of whatever makes that feeling lift. For me, that's taking my dog and my daughter to the park every afternoon and practicing my small talk.

BETHANY: Use your ingenuity; creating change doesn't look the same for all of our communities. A lot of the work has already started so you don't have to reinvent the wheel. Recognize your strengths and contributions and get activated with the like-minded.

KIMBERLY: Don't ask for permission and don't be your first no. It's your life, and no one is going to do the thing that you want to do in the way that you want to do it. Make a commitment to being great and reup on that commitment every single day.

When Fashion and Ac

In a world of fashion and pop-culture media that projects only one vision of beauty and style, there are countless voices and identities left unrepresented. But when two fashion powerhouses came together to celebrate a community that has been underserved and underappreciated, something special happened. Premme was born.

by Grace Bonney

P remme is a new fashion brand that creates bold statement pieces for women sizes 12 to 30. Co-founders Gabi Gregg (better known as GabiFresh to her online fans) and Nicolette Mason met over ten years ago in an online community where fashion bloggers shared their outfits of the day. Connecting over their shared background in activism and a mutual desire to represent and include plus-size women in the fashion industry, they became fast friends. After launching successful collaborative capsule collections with brands like Swimsuitsforall, Target, and ModCloth, Gabi and Nicolette decided to start their own company so they could create without restrictions and design for an audience they knew intimately and better than most designers in the industry.

In 2016, Premme went live with an online collection that was an instant success. And while sales and media buzz were welcomed, what struck the new CEOs most was the feedback and connections they were forming with

Gabi Gregg (this page) and Nicolette Mason (opposite)

tivism Join Together

customers—and members of their community—who felt heard, seen, and appreciated. I sat down to talk with these smart, savvy, and incredibly plugged-in co-founders about how Premme came to be and how they're shaking up the world of fashion—and setting an example for those to come.

How did you first meet each other?

NICOLETTE: I remember the first time I saw Gabi was on a LiveJournal community called "What I Wore Today," or WIWT. It was the first time I saw someone who had a body type more similar to mine than a lot of the other people in the community. We were the same age and I felt instantly drawn to her.

GABI: We were also together in another community called Fatshionista, which was the breeding ground for so many plus-size and body-positive activists today. A lot of us met there. It was one of the first internet communities dedicated to fat positivity, and it taught so many of us about what that meant. It wasn't just about fashion, but it was fashion meets politics.

I remember reaching out to Nicolette and saying, "You should definitely post more photos. I love what you're doing with your style, and we don't see enough of this." That's the first interaction I remember having.

How long into your friendship did you start thinking about starting a business together?

NICOLETTE: In 2009, we met for the first time in real life when Gabi put together the first-ever plus-size bloggers conference. But it wasn't until 2012 that we both thought, "Hey, we should do this together." It was a dream for both of us.

We've both collaborated with other brands, but our vision was so much bigger than what our partners would ever allow us to do. There were just so many limitations in terms of casting and the language that brands use or their size range. Even creatively, our vision was always stifled because other companies had their own ideas about what a plus-size woman does, how she dresses, or what she likes or wants. So we knew that the only way we could really, fully have control over what we wanted was to start something on our own.

Did you ever have any apprehension about working together as friends?

GABI: No. Not at all.

NICOLETTE: There was never any hesitation. I think a big part of it is that we share so much ideologically and politically. We have differences in our styles, and aesthetics, but the things that we share are so much more important. I think it's good to have a little bit of difference and disagreement in terms of style and being able to objectively create things together.

GABI: If Nicolette feels really strongly and I don't, it opens my eyes to the fact that I don't want to get so narrow-minded that I'm dressing or designing things only for myself. You want to have that other perspective.

We also both have equal amounts of experience in the industry, and that makes a huge difference. We've both been doing this for a decade. We both have market experience as editors. We both have been able to build roles within our community. And we also both come from a political background.

So what are your day-to-day roles at the company? Do you have separate roles?

NICOLETTE: We are really good complements to each other and things have worked themselves out organically. I pay all of our contractors and bills from our shared account. Gabi is here in Los Angeles more, so she goes to more of our fittings. But it's not a formal role definition. We really do share all of our responsibilities, and then, on any given day, we're able to balance out our individual needs.

GABI: There are so many hats to be worn, especially with a start-up. We're really small, and there are so many things that need to be done that we both do everything we can, and then it comes down to who has the time that day. We hope as we grow we can bring on more staff members and delegate more easily. But so far I feel like we're both good at everything we've come across.

NICOLETTE: For the last eight years, Gabi and I have been running our own one-person businesses, and so we've had to play all of those roles of administrator, of shipper. Every single thing that we've had to do to run our own businesses as consultants and contractors and market editors has been as individuals. It's very natural for us to go from that to doing a bit of everything at Premme.

What was the most valuable lesson you learned from previous work that you've brought with you to Premme?

NICOLETTE: I think one of the biggest problems for a lot of brands is that they're so stifled by their assumptions about the customer rather than talking to the customer. What has made both Gabi and me so successful in a lot of ways is that we're so connected to our peers, this market and consumer base. Also, we are this consumer, so it's an organic and natural thing for us to be having those conversations and getting really honest feedback. We both have our ears close to the ground in terms of what's happening and what the trends are. I think it's a big mistake when companies view themselves as authorities on communities they're not intimately connected to.

GABI: So many of the brands getting into plus-size fashion are seeing the plus-size customer, especially the confident, stylish plus-size customer, as a trend or a fad. They're trying to figure out a way to insert themselves into this market to capitalize on a hashtag, as opposed to coming from the

> ## Nothing is as perfect as it looks from the outside for anybody.
> *—Nicolette*

1ST ROW (L TO R): @alexmichaelmay, @beautymarked_illy and @kellyaugustineb by @lydiahudgens (2nd and 3rd picture), @thevintagehoneybee, @foreign_curves, @gessflyy by @gossettphotography, @phat_girl_phresh; 2ND ROW (L TO R): @lydiahudgens (1st and 2nd picture), @moorestylemorebeauty, @jennifer.buckingham, @chiefofstyle by @lyvellg, @reztothecity, @nataliemeansnice; 3RD ROW (L TO R): @lydiahudgens (1st and 2nd picture), @hardknockblythe, @itsmekellieb by @lydiahudgens, @roseybeeme by @courtneyjoyphotography (5th and 6th picture), @beautymarked_illy and @thisisjessicatorres by @lydiahudgens (7th and 8th picture); 4TH ROW (L TO R): @littlelimedress, @soshenell by @tahn_jah, @theericalauren, @kellyaugustineb, @ushshi by @lydiahudgens, @premme.us, @alexmichaelmay.

community itself. We know the language because we live the language.

Things like sizing are really important to us. We wanted to come out of the gate doing sizes up to a 30. Because we're starting fresh, we get to decide who we want our customer to be. We want her to be the fashion-forward, risk-taking girl. If she's not that girl yet, we want to encourage those people to take risks. We want to be the brand that's standing out and saying, "We want to push the boundaries, we don't want to play by the rules."

Why do you think established or older brands have struggled to support and celebrate this customer?

GABI: I think a lot of brands have a hard time because they're trying to be everything to everyone. They see the plus-size customer as one customer. But we are just like everyone else. Some of us will want something more modest and some will want bolder statement pieces.

So this idea that one brand can cater to everyone above a certain size is limiting. Things get watered down when you try to please everyone. So instead of imagining all plus-size customers as having the same style, they need to have a vision and embrace that it will work for some, but not all.

How long did that process take you to get the business up and running from an idea to products in packages being mailed out?

NICOLETTE: From the time that Gabi and I said, "Let's do this together," to when we actually hit the market, it was about three and a half years. We had a lot of false starts. We had falling-outs with other business partners. In the beginning, when we were seeking funding, we had a really hard time even getting people to take us seriously because we were two women who didn't have "traditional business experience." We are two plus-size women who, in so many ways, are not traditional in the white, patriarchal, heteronormative way. So people wouldn't even give us face time. We had to bring in our management company, Digital Brand Architects. They started a new division devoted to products and licensing, and they came in as a partner to Premme. Then people started taking us a little bit more seriously.

Starting a business from the ground up is really, really hard. People don't talk about that openly enough. We finally found a great operations partner and manufacturer to handle

manufacturing, technical design, distribution and fulfillment, and customer service. Which has been really helpful. But I think people see that success that we've had so far and the enthusiasm about Premme and think we're raking it in. But this is still a start-up. We're not paying ourselves a single dollar right now. It's going to be a while until we're able to grow our company and bring in staff, but we're committed to doing that because this is such a passion for us. It's also why we're maintaining so many other sides of our businesses right now, so that we can continue to build on this dream and invest back into it as much as we can.

How do you guys take care of yourselves when starting a business can be all-consuming?

NICOLETTE: Honestly, it's been a really big struggle. We've both tried to express that a little bit online so people understand it isn't all easy. Self-care is really hard right now. Gabi and I both have autoimmune issues, so our health is a priority and it needs to be a priority. We both struggle to make time for ourselves and to take care of ourselves, but we're trying our best.

GABI: I have to force it because otherwise it won't get prioritized. I live with mental illness as well, so between physical illness and mental illness, the amount of stress on someone who's trying to run a new business is intense, especially when it's not their only job.

I love Premme, and I want it to be successful, but nothing's more important than living, so I'm going to prioritize that.

So I try to incorporate things like baths and listening to podcasts into my life to calm down a little bit and de-stress. But it's never-ending because the next morning you wake up and you have to do it all over again.

What do your support systems look like?

GABI: My biggest support is my therapist. I wish I could go more than once a week because I look forward to it every week. I'm a really private person, so she's the one person whom I feel comfortable really opening up to. I'm lucky to have friends and family in LA, so that's really nice. But, generally speaking, she's my go-to for the deeper-seated issues.

NICOLETTE: My friends and family have been my biggest supports, and of course Gabi. We spend so much time together that sometimes the only alone time we have is with each other, so we share a lot of these self-support times together.

GABI: A lot of our stresses come from our jobs, and the only person who can really understand how stressful that is is Nicolette. She's going to be the first person I call because she gets it.

NICOLETTE: There are also moments where one of us is frustrated and the other one will say, "It's okay. This is going to work out. We have a plan." I feel so grateful that we have each other in this process because there have been so many tough spots that if we were doing this alone, either of us would've given up. So to have the other to cheerlead and support and rally with has been such an enormous gift to this whole endeavor.

Do you keep a circle of other business owners that you work with and get support from?

GABI: A lot of our friends are entrepreneurs, so that's huge. I didn't come from a family or a place where there were a lot of successful businesspeople. That wasn't in my world. My mom's a teacher. My dad's an artist. So I didn't know entrepreneurs existed besides Mark Cuban or whoever else was on *Shark Tank*. I didn't know what that looked like. But I'm lucky that I've made so many friends my age that are also starting their own businesses. So those are the people I lean on and look to for inspiration.

NICOLETTE: It's been really important for us that we don't really view other people as competition, but rather as a part of a community that we want to grow together. I think having that shift in mind-set has been really, really important for us in building support systems and in building networks of entrepreneurs whom we get to work with because we want everyone to succeed together. It's all shine theory. If I shine, you shine, and there's so much room for all of us to grow and succeed at the same time.

What has been the hardest part about starting this business that you didn't expect?

GABI: Sales are the hardest. You have a great idea, you're so excited about it, and then reality hits when the site goes live. It doesn't sell itself, no matter how many fans you have. Ultimately you have to make things that people actually buy. We can't just make them because we love them. So that's changing a bit of how I see our business. That, for me, has been the hardest lesson, just to realize, okay, it's not just a passion project. It has to make money, too.

What's been one of the best things that's maybe surprised you, that you didn't expect to feel?

NICOLETTE: I think just seeing the immediate enthusiasm and support of our community and how excited people are to wear the clothes and to get them in the mail. People are posting on Instagram as soon as they receive their package and they're so excited to participate in it. Premme has also been mentioned alongside brands that have been around for decades as industry leaders. So for us to be seen as peers of brands that have literally decades of experience and millions of dollars in support is really incredible and affirming. We just want to exceed those expectations and keep growing, being the best that we can.

How are you integrating social media feedback into your business?

NICOLETTE: The enthusiasm around our striped jumpsuit that we launched with is a great example. The response was so incredible that we decided to keep the style going with more colors. We post things on Instagram Stories to see what people want to see made or what additions they want to existing pieces. That's such valuable and immediate feedback.

GABI: We're both really involved in Premme's social media as customer service, too. We're answering DMs. We're in the comments. We are there seeing what people are saying. If they have feedback, good or bad, we want to respond to it and take it into our next meeting and say, "Okay, people are saying this arm doesn't fit right. What can we do to make sure this doesn't happen next time?"

What effect do you hope Premme will have on the fashion community as a whole?

NICOLETTE: This might be controversial, but I don't think every brand should get in to the plus-size market just to do it. I think it has to be organic and not just about adding on to their sizes but for them to actually be thoughtful about the way they do it, to use plus-size fit models and grade off of those sizes instead of just adding inches to a size 6. So I would hope that any brand that wants to grow into this market will be committed to doing it right and not treating it as an afterthought or an add-on.

We deserve to have more and better options. Part of the reason we started Premme was because there are only about five places that a fashion-forward young person who fits above a size 12 can shop. So I really welcome any brand that wants to invest in this market, but I hope they will do it well and with respect.

GABI: We've heard for our entire careers that plus-size women don't want stylish clothing and that it won't sell. But we are going against that because we believe it needs to be done—and done well.

We hope that if we show people how to do it right, from the ground up, that we can prove that this community can be a powerful force in the buying community. I hope that along with Premme, and brands like ASOS and Eloquii, some of the old-school straight-size brands will pay attention and invest in designing for more people.

What's your dream expansion for your business if you got the funding, growth, and sales that you wanted? Where do you see this growing?

NICOLETTE: Our vision has always been pretty conservative. We want to grow organically and slowly and allow time to get everything right. We want to be a destination for plus-size shoppers. When someone has a special event or wants just really cool clothes to fill out their wardrobe, we want Premme to be the first place they go. Down the line we'd love to do accessories: lingerie, shoes, jewelry. Bridal is even a place that we've thought about. Our community needs accessible, cool bridal gowns. There are so many opportunities for growth in this market that it's kind of limitless, but we don't want to grow too fast, too soon.

You've both talked about the idea of body positive sometimes being synonymous with plus-size bodies being sexualized and how to counteract that but still include that as an option. How do you handle that when you're dealing with styling and models?

NICOLETTE: That's something that's always been an either/or. You're either hypersexualized or you're a completely nonsexual object because how could you possibly be a sexual object? There haven't been options to exist as both or as in-between or any of that. So we're trying to provide as many options as possible.

It sometimes feels like there's this pressure to either be super sexy and if you're not, you're not body positive enough. But you don't have to participate in hypersexualization in order to love yourself. You can love your body and love who you are and choose how to dress yourself. That's really the whole crux of it for me, that people should just have the choice to dress how they want.

GABI: We want to give people the option to talk about style first. That's what Premme is about. Fashion first. Yes, we do have some sexy pieces, and that's great, but it's not about dressing only to have sex appeal or to be sexually attractive. It's about what's in and what's trending. Is it oversize? Cool. That's awesome. We can wear oversize, shapeless stuff, too. It's not about hiding. It's just about what's cute. There's no reason a thin woman can wear an oversize, shapeless sack and I can't. There's a difference between doing it because you want to hide and doing it because it's stylish and cool.

What do you want younger fans and customers to know as they look to you for guidance and as role models?

NICOLETTE: I think it's important for people to recognize that every single person has something they're insecure about. Even the people who others perceive as perfect and having it all—they are struggling with something. People think that about us, that our lives are perfect, and they're not. We have bad days in terms of body image. We have bad days in terms of mental health. We have just bad days. Nothing is as perfect as it looks from the outside for anybody. So to recognize that we all have our struggles and it's okay to have those struggles and we'll all get through them is a really, really important thing for me.

What's your favorite thing about your business partner, and why are you so thankful for that part of them?

NICOLETTE: I know I can be so tremendously honest with Gabi, and I can tell her anything, whether it's about each other or about personal lives or business. I can trust her with anything and also trust myself to be honest with her.

GABI: I have to say transparency and honesty. I feel like so many business partners aren't that way with each other. But we're honest and open with each other and I'm so grateful that I can be that way with Nicolette and she doesn't make me feel bad about it.

NICOLETTE: We know each other's histories inside and out and we deeply appreciate each other for who we are.

> I love Premme, and I want it to be successful, but nothing's more important than living, so I'm going to prioritize that first. —*Gabi*

RESHAPING THE MEDIA

by Nora Gomez-Strauss

In recent years, women have been encouraged to
"take a seat at the table." But, what happens when there are no
seats left? Sometimes the first step is making your own table.
Writer Nora Gomez-Strauss talks to three women
leading the fight for equity in media representation while creating
their own platforms for underrepresented communities.

For generations, mainstream media has catered to and represented a homogenous portion of the public. As our country continues to become more diverse, its people and stories still struggle to be represented on a broader scale. However, thanks to those who take the "If it's to be, it's up to me" mantra to heart, that has begun to change in the past decade. Women are taking leadership in creating spaces for the voices that otherwise have nowhere to be heard.

Pioneering publications like *Ebony*, *Ms.*, and *Out*, have planted seeds for new media outlets to create their own paths; however, as the print-to-digital changeover took place, representation and inclusiveness seemed to get further left behind. Then, with the 2000s came new voices. In 2008, *Remezcla* emerged, representing modern Latinx. Editor in chief Andrea Gompf recalls hearing about the publication for the first time: "I completely fell in love with its fresh voice and perspective. Before that, I'd never encountered a publication that spoke to me as a young, US-born Latina." The next year, *Autostraddle* became the smart (and very funny) go-to for the feminist

LGBTQ community. "When I was thirteen or so and like wildly depressed and full of self-loathing in that special adolescent way, I promised myself if I lived into adulthood, I would dedicate my life to helping girls feel better about themselves," says *Autostraddle*'s Riese Bernard. And finally, *The Mash-Up Americans* has become the face of how we look at the traditional American family. Founder Amy Choi says it best: "By telling stories and having conversations, we build empathy and help the people see those who are different from them as equally human to them."

An ideal all three women share is the desire to ensure that people do not feel alone, that we all have a place to turn, no matter who we are. These publications go beyond their articles and act as spaces where people can be themselves. They serve as online communities of shared visions and values. At the same time, it is impossible to discuss this without mentioning the challenges that lie ahead. There is still so much work to be done, but luckily, with leaders in media like these, it does not seem too far out of reach. What is "inclusive" and "diverse" today may just become "normal" tomorrow.

RIESE BERNARD

Co-founder, Editor in Chief,
CEO, CFO, Autostraddle

Growing up loving magazines, Riese Bernard was scheming up ideas similar to *Teen Vogue* before it even existed. Later on in her adult life, she became wrapped up in the beginnings of the blog world, and her side-blog dedicated to *The L Word* recaps led to collaborations with Showtime, among others. The blog also led her to create a community of like-minded queer women in New York City. It was through this group that she met her then-girlfriend Alex Vega, who would become *Autostraddle*'s co-founder. They saw the lack of pressing topics covered by traditional media and sought to fill the gap, but with a focus on gay women. They tackled issues like mental health right away, and the response was powerful. "I was consistently blown away and touched getting emails from blog readers who said my work had helped them get through this or that." As *The L Word* winded down, *Autostraddle* came into its own, with full-time dedication. There was nothing else quite like it out there, and Riese made it her mission to create the space so many needed. "Basically, I wanted to be an editor in chief and I didn't have the patience or the connections to climb the ladder at an existing publication, so I made my own."

How has *Autostraddle* changed over the course of its existence?

"How hasn't it changed?" would probably be easier to answer! The world and the online media landscape have changed radically, so we've changed in turn—we used to be one of only a few places readers could find LGBTQ-related news, there were only a few out queer celebrities, and lesbian characters on television were even rarer than they are now. We wrote about Lady Gaga, *Glee*, and Adam Lambert approximately every day, a choice I cannot necessarily defend, but I promise it made perfect sense at the time. We've gone from posting about same-sex marriage legislation to doing features on same-sex wedding attire, you know? We're bigger and more diverse, we now have editors on salary and pay all our writers and artists. Taking our publication into 3-D with the launch of A-Camp (an annual summer camp for the LGBTQIA community) was another huge shift—it connected us to our readers in a very tangible and transformative way.

Do you see the role of *Autostraddle* as having changed in the past year?

Yes, but we're still sorting that out. I think we've posited ourselves as a refuge almost by default—we don't have any reporters, so keeping up with the daily barrage of terrible news got real futile real fast—a place where people otherwise emotionally terrorized by the present moment can take a breath, knowing that they're surrounded by people who care exactly as much as they do and will fight for them. Things feel . . . dark. Out there in the world. Very dark. We want to be a part of the resistance, actively, and every day we're looking to our community for how to best harness our resources toward that cause.

What do you want your readers to take away?

That they're not alone. That whatever is weird or different about them is okay and there are other people out there who share those differences and that weirdness. That they're doing okay. That they can define who they are for themselves, that there's no singular way to be a woman or to be a lesbian or to be queer or to be trans or to be whatever they are. That it's okay to be a little crazy and stretch marks are hot and books are cool. It'd be neat if they learned a little history, too. Gotta know where you've been to know where you're going, etc.

What are your short-term goals for *Autostraddle*?
To do more feature stories and original reporting. We recently got a financial gift from the estate of Jeanne Córdova, an incredible lesbian journalist who started the *Lesbian Tide* in the '70s and was an activist all her life, who passed away from cancer in January 2016, and although most of that has gone into maintaining our current operations, we're looking to funnel some of it into commissioning experienced reporters to do long-form feature journalism for us. We need more women of color on the senior editors team. We're always, always, always aiming for more racial diversity. Also, health insurance!

How do you see it evolving over the next decade? What life do you see it having beyond your tenure?
I think by 2027, everybody will be gay, so none of this will matter. Alternatively, I see us expanding the A-Camp wing and developing other live events that enable our readers to find community in real life and connect with the incredible talent in our network. We'd like to partner with smaller groups and publications focused on QTPOC (Queer Trans People of Color) to bring that work to a larger audience and get more funding for it. I wanna bring back the *Autostraddle* Calendar Girls but with a specific focus on ambassadors/activists. We'd like to launch an original video series—we have so many talented friends doing incredible work that deserves sponsorship and a showcase, but we will never "pivot to video," my friends. I want a literary salon like Natalie Barney's. There are a lot of community features.

I think we're getting to a point where raising investment capital is looking more viable/necessary—we're doing what we can with what we have but when Condé Nast announced they were starting an LGBTQ magazine, their first new title launch in many years, we were kind of shell-shocked, like, "How will we keep up with this?"

So what happens over the next decade depends entirely on finances. We don't take any of this for granted.

Although *Autostraddle* was created for the feminist LGBTQ+ community, do you hope those outside of that community are paying attention to the dialogues you're creating and furthering?
I hope that those within the feminist LGBTQ+ community are empowered and educated by the dialogues we're creating in a way that enables them to communicate effectively with those outside of the community. A chunk of queer women came of age with *Autostraddle* and are out because of our work, and that has a giant radiating effect like a virus—but good.

We certainly don't write for those outside the community, but we have lots of readers who visit regularly to better relate to their LGBTQ+ friends and family, which's touching. Often we have a piece go viral that exposes wide swaths of humans to complicated queer and trans issues, which is surreal and great.

How do you stay inspired?
Very early in *Autostraddle*'s existence I still was working a few other jobs. I remember the first day I woke up knowing that all I had on the agenda for that day was *Autostraddle*, and it was the best feeling in the world. I want to create things and learn things and connect with people, and I finally had an outlet for the six thousand ideas constantly screaming at me from the back of my brain. As *Autostraddle* kept developing, those mornings I woke up having to go to a different job got heavier and heavier. So I try to never forget that feeling, and what it used to be like when I woke up not knowing I'd have an entire day to create things and connect with people.

I keep meaningful letters from readers—usually letters/notes left for me at A-Camp from readers who came to camp—over my desk. I have an amazing, incredible team and I read a lot, especially a lot of lesbian history and the history of queer media.

I love bringing new people onto the team and being exposed to new viewpoints and perspectives. Truly, I've never lacked for inspiration. Time and money, on the other hand, are in very short supply.

ab   ×

← → C   🔒 Secure | https://www.autostraddle.com

(A S) **AUTOSTRADDLE**

A+   ARTS & POP CULTURE   SEX & DATING   POLITICS   COMMUNITY   COLUMNS   IDENTITIES   MORE ☰

AMY S. CHOI

Co-founder and Editorial Director,
The Mash-Up Americans

Being the first of her family born in the United States, Amy Choi has always felt she was a part of multiple worlds. She was a Korean daughter, an American student feminist, and an English/Korean/Spanish speaker—a true "mash-up" before she and co-founder Rebecca Lehrer coined the term. Amy fell in love with another first-gener, making a Korean-Colombian-Mexican family together. "My life navigating all of these identities has always been complicated and challenging and rich and amazing," Amy says of her family and friends who are on the same journey. It was a natural friendship when she met Rebecca, another mash-up. Recognizing that there was no media focusing on the new, multicultural-identity family, the two decided to make a company on their own. Eight years into their friendship, *The Mash-Up Americans* was born.

How has *MUA* changed over the course of its existence?

Honestly, its mission and our vision haven't changed that much in five years. We have a mini-retreat every six months and a larger one at the beginning of every year, when we reflect on what we've accomplished and set priorities and goals for the six months, one year, two years ahead. It's a time for soul-searching—What has been our impact? How do we measure impact? Have we stayed true to our mission? Has our mission shifted? What do we want from this beast we've created? Are we personally still experiencing joy and fulfillment from this work? And we are always somewhat surprised when we see how consistent we have been, in the editorial, creative, business, and mission, since the very beginning. *The Mash-Up Americans* exists to elevate often-ignored voices, recenter the American narrative on our experience of it, and celebrate and support our noisy, raucous, challenging, multicultural brethren. By telling stories and having conversations, we build empathy and help people see those who are different from them as equally human to them. What has changed is the context in which we live

and operate. Since November 9, 2016, we see our work not just as a celebration, but as a cause.

Do you see the role of *MUA* as having changed in the past year?

Though Rebecca and I have always been advocates in our personal lives, we are much more explicitly political and socially active as a business than we were in the early days of *Mash-Up*. Listen, our core principle is optimism. Not a "rose-colored-glasses-everything-will-be-okay" optimism, but a deep belief that we as individuals and as a community can come together to create a more just, more empathetic world that is a little less broken than the one we entered into. Like the Jewish idea of *tikkun olam*—that we have the power to repair the world in some way. We understand that our community feels deeply afraid and deeply angry right now, and we do, too. Our role now, in addition to what we've always done in terms of amplifying our community voices, is to help support them in their work to repair the world. Sometimes that means curating political and social justice resources; sometimes it means offering a safe place to vent; sometimes it means making our people laugh.

What do you want your readers/listeners to take away?

That you have permission to be your whole self—all of your identities—and that you are enough. That you don't have to pass an authenticity test with us, or with anyone. That being your whole complex self and drawing from all of your traditions and making that self heard in the world is incredibly valuable. That it's good to ask questions and be questioning, and that you can ask nearly any awkward, difficult question as long as you do it with compassion and humor. That you are not alone.

What are your short-term goals for MUA?

To become media mogul billionaires! I'm going to Oprah-*Secret* that very short-term future into existence. Also, we are working hard to deepen and dramatically expand our podcast audience; keep experimenting with innovative ways to engage with the community and meet people where they are; and continue building our creative studio, which supports our editorial work and brings *The Mash-Up Americans* to large organizations to help them think in a more nuanced way about how to center the *Mash-Up* customer. How can companies redefine the "we" and the "they"? How can brands engage deeply on our more universally lived experiences, rather than thinking about verticals of race and identity? How do we get Mash-Ups out of the ethnic aisle? We want to bring *Mash-Up* thinking and questioning into the very, very, very beginning of the design process.

How do you see it evolving over the next decade? What life do you see it having beyond your tenure?

Honestly, wouldn't it be incredible to see *Mash-Up* become obsolete? That "diverse" (ugh, we hate that word sometimes) subjects and issues become a central part of the national conversation, and not a vertical adjacent to the mainstream? That we see each other all as full humans? I look forward to that day!

Though it's always hard to know how we'll evolve creatively, strategically, we see *The Mash-Up Americans* growing into a large, multifaceted media organization that leads the conversation on identity in America while it supports and develops professional and creative women, especially women of color; immigrants; the LGBTQIA community; and marginalized communities as a whole. We do this already in a micro way as a small business, and we expect to do it in a massive macro way in the future.

Any successors passionate about *Mash-Up* will be equally committed to it. As proud as we are of our creative work and community building, we are equally proud of the microeconomy we have created around *The Mash-Up Americans* and the number of women we have been able to employ in different capacities. They are the beating heart of *Mash-Up,* and as long as they thrive, *Mash-Up* will, too.

Although MUA was created to address the experience of those with different ethnic backgrounds, do you hope those outside of that community are paying attention to the dialogues you're creating and furthering?

One thousand bazillion percent yes. And they are. Each of our different editorial platforms has a slightly different audience—in our Venn diagram of newsletter, website, and podcast, only a small minority, our superuser, engages regularly with all three—but our weekly newsletter, in which we curate news with a *Mash-Up* lens, in particular, has a disproportionately large audience of white women. Our in-box is a mix of "Thank God I found you; I'm this-this-this-that, and I thought I was all alone in the world." In the custom content we create for our partners—for example, we produced an online audio conference with The MIT Media Lab and Automattic on design and exclusion in the tech industry—we absolutely are creating work with an understanding that many of the participants aren't our traditional demographic. But we don't chase that audience. There's enough out there for white people! We center ourselves, our identities, and our issues. A surprising discovery was realizing that the more we stay true to that, the more universally relatable and emotionally effective our storytelling is, both to people outside the community and to those Mash-Ups who might not share any of the same hyphens. Once we have that connection, the conversations and the work can go so much further.

How do you stay inspired?

Sometimes I see my kids make art for the people they care about, or make music, or create characters. I watch them create imaginary worlds for themselves and it's like love starts pinballing around in my body, like on a cellular level. My skin tingles and all I can think about is how I never, ever, ever want them to stop creating, or to stop believing that they have the power to create the world they want to live in. I want them to know that they can help repair the world. So I am continually inspired to do my part, too.

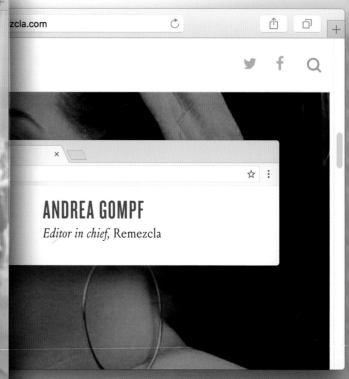

ANDREA GOMPF

Editor in chief, Remezcla

T he recession that gripped the country in 2008 did not exactly give Andrea Gompf the media opportunities she was hoping for when she moved to New York City. Taking a position at an immigration law firm, she continued to freelance write in her spare time. While she was out one evening in Williamsburg, the sounds of global bass and digital cumbia caught her ear. Andrea befriended the DJs behind the music, who had also started a known party on the Latino scene, Que Bajo?! They would then introduce her to *Remezcla,* a publication unlike anything she had read before. Becoming enamored with its fresh take, she made getting a job there her goal. After hitting refresh on their careers page continually to no avail, she sent a heartfelt email explaining why they should hire her. That gutsy email led to an interview that led to a position as city editor, and the rest is history.

How has *Remezcla* changed over the course of its existence?
Remezcla has been around for more than ten years, and in that time a lot has changed in the media landscape and in the culture at large.

In its earliest iteration, *Remezcla* was an email newsletter that clued people in to great events in the Latino cultural underground—emerging music, arts, nightlife, etc. That newsletter expanded from New York City to Los Angeles, San Francisco, Chicago, and Miami, and eventually it evolved into a blog with event calendars (kind of like *Time Out New York,* but with a focus on Latino culture). Then, in 2014, we relaunched the site with multiple new verticals, including music, film, food, sports, and culture. We've definitely expanded the subject matter we cover over the years, but our mission has always remained the same: to give young Latinos in the United States a voice, and to tell great stories about a new generation that is evolving what Latino culture looks like.

What do you want your readers to take away?
I hope they leave inspired by the richness and diversity of what Latino culture has to offer. We want to be a place where people can feel connected to and proud of their heritage, while also encouraging them to imagine new, more expansive ways to think about what that identity means.

December 7, 2017
New Music

Miguel's "Now" Video Is a Powerful Stateme[nt]
Injustice of Immigrant Detention

Do you see the role of *Remezcla* as having changed in the past year?

Definitely. Our nation—one that was built with the contributions of Latinos who came to the United States at different times in its history (and some who were here before the Unoted States even existed)—is facing a difficult challenge. It is now helmed by a man who was ushered into office on the promise of toxic nationalism, white supremacy, misogyny, and homophobia. His presidency has unleashed a lot of bigotry and hate into the political mainstream. In this political climate, we are more committed than ever to creating a safe space for young Latinos, a place that reminds them that they have value, and that reaffirms that our communities have always been and will continue to be essential parts of shaping and redefining this country's future. Now more than ever, Latinos have to come together as a community, support each other, hold each other accountable. Telling great stories about who we are and who we can be is part of that work.

What are your short-term goals for *Remezcla*?

To continue growing! There are so many great stories out there to tell, and I think we're only scratching the surface of what we can do. Also, we moved into a new office that has an event space, and I'm really excited to roll out a killer events program for 2018 that brings our readers/ community in to experience *Remezcla* IRL.

How do you see it evolving over the next decade? What life do you see it having beyond your tenure as editor in chief?

I want *Remezcla* to change the way the world sees Latinos. I can see the brand expanding into any space that helps drive and define culture: making TV shows, movies, written content; launching music and film festivals; designing apparel; etc.

I also want it to be a place that launches the careers of new Latino talent. Latinos are underrepresented in newsrooms across the country for many reasons. Many do not have the financial support or access to the same types of networks that allow for unpaid internships or important job referrals. I think *Remezcla* has an opportunity to give young Latinos a foot in the door, and training that they may not be able to get elsewhere.

Although *Remezcla* was created to cover new stories in Latin culture, do you hope those outside of that community are paying attention to the dialogues you're creating and furthering?

Absolutely! We want the whole world to pay attention.

How do you stay inspired?

I am most inspired when in the company of creative people—from all industries, backgrounds, and walks of life.

The Changing Face of Stock Photography

Stock photography is a huge part of our everyday lives. It surrounds us everywhere we go, online and off.

by Rebekah Carey

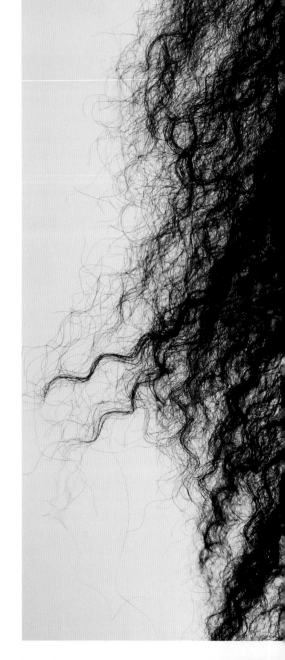

At first glance these images may seem innocuous, but the pervasiveness of white, heteronormative, and able-bodied narratives is overwhelming. And the messages these photos send have less to do with representation and inclusivity than they do with reinforcing the notion that the people being represented are the ones that matter most.

Representation matters at every level of media production, and when members of our community aren't shown—or thought of—as viable examples of "businesswomen" or "happiness," the larger message being sent is deeply problematic. And while mainstream stock photo companies have a long way to go, there are some companies working to change the way we see (literally) ourselves in photography as a whole.

Photographer Brittani Sensabaugh (aka Brittsense) takes photos of people in overlooked, underappreciated, and often misrepresented neighborhoods like East Oakland, the Third Ward of Houston, and Compton. Her goal is to give a voice and face to people who are too commonly represented negatively in the media.

Along with individual documentarians and photo journalists like Brittani, there is a growing wave of independent companies working to increase representation of people of color through stock photography. One of those companies is CreateHER Stock, which focuses on creating positive images of women of color. I sat down with Brittani Sensabaugh and Neosha Gardner of CreateHER Stock to talk about the importance of the work they're doing and how we can support it as consumers and producers of media.

Brittani Sensabaugh

Brittsense

Brittani, what inspired you to pursue photojournalism?
Ever since I was little I've seen and experienced life in pictures. I've always been someone who felt the pain of people around me, but also the love. My main mission when I'm documenting communities is to help them build better foundations. I want to bring back the awareness and unconditional love we lack within these communities so that we're all able to prosper. I consider

myself a documentarian because it's bigger than just "taking pictures." I'm creating a blueprint and archives that will live on for future generations.

In addition to creating your own media company, you also created and raised your own empowering billboards throughout your community. And recently you published your first book. For those who may not be familiar with your work, which of these projects came first and how did it lead you to creating the inspiring community that exists around your work?
For my "222ForgottenCities" project, I traveled the world and documented ten cities where people of color live. These are places the media talks down to (and about), and during that project I realized I needed to create my own media channel. What motivated and inspired me was the fact that so many of my people would go to my Instagram feed or my website every day. They told me they would look at the moments I've captured and feel uplifted to see the beauty of their existence reflected. I thought to myself how I could spread those same feelings and vibrations into other spaces. That lead to creating my billboards.

Advertisements are something I've become attracted to because I feel like we are controlled by them physiologically. When you see most billboards, they're usually selling something that keeps you in an illusion and a capitalist mentality. With my billboards I wanted to try to heal my people by having them see themselves. My focus is on eating healthy and nourishing their existence physically and mentally, so they can build prosperous foundations in the areas where there is nothing but destruction and distractions. When I created my book, *Power of Melanin,* my mission was the same: to provide nourishment, healing, unconditional love, and, most important, to look at the root of your existence so you're able to deal with trauma and triggers.

You self-financed billboards you've created that highlight the beauty of black communities. What have people's reactions been to them?
For two of my billboards I used photographs of local children from that community, so it was impactful to see the strong response from their family and others. When

they looked up at the billboard and saw themselves and smiled, it really put into perspective how much I needed to create more of these billboards. We read and see messaging daily on what we need to buy, but there is rarely any messaging that tells us that loving yourself unconditionally and being healthy is a revolutionary act. We all need to move more out of intention and less from habit.

People who've seen these billboards in their community told me it feels refreshing and liberating to see them, because we are so used to seeing ourselves portrayed in such a negative light. These billboards help us focus on the positive and tap into the power within us.

When you launched your own media company, 222 Media, what did you hope to achieve and what did you hope to change within the media world?
I wanted to create a media company that would help guide future generations. There are limited spaces, resources, and outlets where we can share our narrative in a way that uplifts us and shows our existence the way we feel it should be shown. I wanted to do this through documentation, but I also wanted to create a platform where more of my people could share their perspective with others. This company is a way for us to build together and not be separated from our own energy. For generations someone else has told our narratives. Now it's time to tell our own.

In addition to a lack of fair and accurate representation, what do you feel mainstream media gets wrong in stock photography that more people need to understand?
I feel like mainstream media creates stereotypes based on the system they have created for us. Most of the time when you see someone "black" in the mainstream media, they're being exploited or shown in a negative light. I feel like we are still the outsiders in this society when in reality we built this country with our own hands. There needs to be more of that shown than us being depicted as savages and poverty-stricken people.

What do you hope your new book, *The Power Of Melanin,* offers to its readers?
Melanin is a pigment found in the body of humans, plants, and animals that is responsible for the color of hair, skin, and eyes. Melanin is more than a color, though; it is a key identifier. My book looks at how melanin expresses itself in both our people and the plants and fruits of the earth, showing our connection with nature and the planet. My mission with the book is to plant seeds of love and nourishment so we can all grow and feel confident doing it. I want my people to feel this not because of what society says beauty is or isn't, but because they can actually feel and see that beauty within themselves.

You've built a strong community through Instagram with your work. How has Instagram helped to foster your message of empowering community?
In many ways I'm an introvert, so social media can be bittersweet. Overall, Instagram has been a beautiful way for me to spread this movement. I'm very aware of how powerful energy can be, so I try to make sure I maintain a balance of being present in the online world, but not to the point where it consumes my existence. When I'm on any social platform, I make sure my audience feels love.

Do you have any advice for people who want to nurture community and pride in their own neighborhoods?
Always remember that what makes you most powerful is that there is only one of you on this earth. Your perspective is worthy beyond the walls that society has built to make you feel like it isn't. Create your own pace and realize that all moments are a process. You won't be able to master your journey and mission in one day. Take time to breathe, heal, and nourish yourself first so you can spread that same energy to others. You can't change anyone, but you can plant seeds that can inspire growth.

What advice do you have about funding and/or support for women who would like to start businesses and projects like yours?
Don't measure your success by what society says. Creating projects that are rooted in love and that inspire people to be themselves is automatic success and people will gravitate toward that. Build your own community so on days when you feel defeated, you have a space that offers genuine support and reassurance.

Neosha Gardner
CreateHER Stock

You have created an incredible company that celebrates and provides high-quality, inclusive stock photography. What led you to this project and what was the tipping point that started it?

One day I was struggling with a blog post of mine that required a very specific type of image that I couldn't seem to find anywhere. So, I took to the web to see if there was any platform that offered the type of images I needed. But there was nothing. Or at least nothing that was as engaging as I hoped. That alone made me question why no one had thought to create and execute a platform tailored to women of color. I saw this moment as an opportunity to solve that issue.

What type of clients typically approach you for images for their companies?

We get users and clients from all walks of life and cultures. Although we tailor to black women in general, we have people of other ethnicities who share the struggle of finding good, quality stock imagery. We hear from small firms all the way up to big agencies.

How do you help clients understand why it's so important to be more inclusive and accurately represent communities they're hoping to reach?

First off, by making sure they understand their own audiences. If they're trying to reach a different demographic of people, I always say they should first consult with someone of that demographic. We all interconnect in ways only we can grasp. Go to the source and start from there to learn how to best represent them within your niche.

In what ways do you feel consumers can support (or demand) stock photography that is more representational of a broader audience?

They can request it and pitch ideas to marketing teams. Whomever they're supporting should always be willing to take note of what their consumers

want. If not, consumers should either boycott or stop supporting those companies altogether.

People may not initially realize how far-reaching something like stock photography can be by only representing a sliver of races and other messages like heteronormative gender roles and abilities. How does more thoughtful stock photography change that narrative?
The inclusion of more than just the "typical" would benefit us all greatly. There is a great need for stock images that relate to the LGBTQ and differently abled communities. Anyone who has a personal connection to those communities, and others, should take the lead and create the platforms for

those images as well. Representation in stock photography shows a sign of respect to those being represented. It can signal that people, companies, and other businesses are listening and paying attention. Done right, more inclusive representation can create bigger rewards in the long run.

What do you see for the future of stock photography and where would you like to see your businesses grow?
I hope to see even more genres of modern stock imagery. I'd like to see the inclusion of more than just "man, woman, and child," you know? I'd love to see my business as one of the leading platforms for stock imagery for bloggers of all types. We've really built something special.

WOMEN WHO DRAW

What began as an idea to build a website that helped increase the visibility of female, LGBTQ+, and marginalized illustrators turned into a world of opportunity. Not just for paying jobs, but for collaboration, connection, and community.

by Lostboy

As someone who identifies as a queer Korean American gender-nonconforming artist with depression, space and attention are not a given. It is not easily handed over, nor is it expected. In fact, POC artists are routinely overlooked, undervalued, silenced, and in most cases, invisible. But there is a revolutionary movement growing and the roots are deep within the creative community. People are acknowledging the ways in which privilege goes hand in hand with the amount of opportunity and exposure one gets. This is why visibility is so important, especially in the creative community. And this is why I'm so proud that Women Who Draw exists.

Women Who Draw was created by artists Julia Rothman and Wendy MacNaughton as a way to bring attention to women (WWD is trans-inclusive and includes women, trans, and gender-nonconforming illustrators) in the illustration community. After noticing the lack of women being hired for editorial work, they decided to create a place where people looking to hire artists could easily find someone talented. It also served as a quick and easy way for companies avoid the same excuse we've heard before that they simply "couldn't find anyone" who was female, LGBTQ+, Muslim, etc., to hire.

Instantly, I fell in love with the idea of creating a space for women of all different backgrounds to be showcased for exactly that—our differences. In those differences, I found a community. It's a struggle to find underrepresented artists in the abyss we call social media, so to be able to selectively seek out creatives who self-identify in the same spectrum (i.e., queer/Asian/Californian) has been a gem of a resource.

I was lucky enough to be asked to experience the beta website before it went live and to work with Julia and Wendy on the first round of feedback from a wide range of artists. They recognized the huge responsibility that exists, especially in the current climate, to create any type of platform that is accessible and respectful of people from all different identities.

In my experience as an artist, there is a huge disconnect between the people doing the hiring (art directors, companies, publications) and the people hoping to be hired. But Women Who Draw set out to bridge that gap and I was hopeful. And one week after the website went live, I heard from the *New York Times*. They let me know they'd found me through the website and I was able to get an illustration into the Christmas edition of the paper. It felt amazing to submit an illustration and a few keywords and then find myself with such an incredible opportunity. And while these opportunities are great, what's even better is to have found a community. There is nothing more beautiful than women empowering women. I am encouraged every time I see the hashtag #womenwhodraw online because I know this is where hopeful creatives put themselves out there, to be seen and to be visible to our shared community.

I invited some fellow artists from our community to share their work and talk about what a resource like this means to them and how it's changed the landscape of women in illustration.

NYANZA D

nyanzad.com
@nyanzad_

Since being featured on the WWD directory, I've done collaborations with artists like Saint Rose, Rinny Riot, and Xavier Payne and I'd love to do more. A site like this is so important because a lot of female artists are overlooked. The website has very specific categories, so if you're a client looking for an artist from a particular background, then it's much easier to find them. For example, if you're looking for a black female artist from Europe, then you'd find artists like me or Ojima Abalaka. I have discovered an array of artists and it's opened my eyes not only to the range of artistic styles, but also to how many identities people use for themselves and how that shapes their work.

LOVEIS WISE

loveiswise.com
@cosmicsomething @LoveisWise_

My experience with Women Who Draw has been amazing, to say the least. I've met so many talented folks from the platform and it has honestly changed my career in so many positive ways. Many of my clients have noted that they had discovered my work through the site and I've gained some pretty cool collaborations and friendships through WWD. A resource like this is so important because it gives a space and opportunity to a diverse group of women trying to put themselves and their work out in the world. This platform made so many female-identified illustrators visible in a white cisgender male–dominated industry.

HERIKITA

cargocollective.com
@herikitaconk

**Why do you feel a site like
WWD is so important?**
It's an amazing site. Everyone is so
talented. It's an incredible directory that's
making a real difference. Being a woman in
illustration is an important role because
you are telling people your story and how
it is to live in the world.

NISHAT AKHTAR

nishatakhtar.com
@nishat

I've had people contact me for illustration jobs through WWD, but the biggest and greatest experience is having so much exposure to womxn illustrators, especially of color. As a first-generation Indian American brown woman, the longing for visibility and amplification of POC voices in art, has been a dire thirst for my entire lifetime. On this site you can find a diverse group of artists creating all kinds of work and I've spent a lot of downtime discovering new sheroes to follow. It's also so refreshing and validating to see different kinds of bodies (shapes, colors, and personalities) so richly represented in illustrators' work. This site acts like a powerful signal boost to this huge (and growing) community and is amplifying accessibility to all of these artists.

MARÍA LUQUE

cargocollective.com/marialuque

@maria.j.luque

Projects like WWD are really important so we, artists and art directors, can realize how many amazing, talented women, trans, and gender-nonconforming illustrators there are out in the world working. Not only does it give visibility to our community, but it helps dismantle the idea that women are competing with each other. It's exactly the opposite—there are so many of us working together and that is powerful.

ALEXANDRA BOWMAN

alexandrabowman.com
@alexandrabowmanart

I have made so many connections, have been involved in collaborations, and have gotten several jobs from WWD. A resource like this gives women more visibility and, in turn, better opportunity for jobs. It is so empowering to be seen and to see women around the world hustling and creating beautiful work. This is an online community of women who support not just each other, but also the entire network of female business owners seeking illustrators to hire.

DAIANA RUIZ

daianaruiz.tumblr.com
@dai.ruiz

To be part of Women Who Draw is very important to me. Through this website and community I've made several collaborations and I have gotten to know a lot of women who make beautiful illustrations around the world. For me it's really important that this site is so inclusive. It provides solidarity and visibility, which are fundamental for making a future based on equality and social justice for all.

Author and bookstore owner Emma Straub talks to women who are changing the world of bookstores.

never planned to open a bookstore. It was something that my husband and I talked about from time to time. More specifically, we talked about taking over for the owners of our local bookstore (BookCourt in Brooklyn, New York) when they wanted to retire. We talked about it as seriously as we talked about going to Hawaii someday, or getting matching tattoos: a nice idea that would probably never happen. But then things did happen, and fast—when I was seven months pregnant with our second child, we moved as close as we could to BookCourt. A year later, it closed. We had a plan to open a new store immediately.

The very first thing I did was write an "Am I crazy?" email to Ann Patchett, novelist and owner of Parnassus Books; I then called my friend Christine Onorati, who owns a bookstore, WORD, with three locations. As a former bookseller and a novelist, I knew some of what went into having a bookstore—the endless stream of boxes, the constant alphabetizing, the meetings with sales reps from publishers, the ragtag teams of smart booksellers, always happy to wax rhapsodic about their latest read. There was a lot I didn't know—a lot we didn't know—but none of it deterred us, not for a second.

In the industry, we call wide swaths of land (urban, suburban, rural) without bookstores "book deserts." I live in Brooklyn, which is whatever the opposite of a book desert is. There are WORD, Community Bookstore, Greenlight Bookstore, Stories Bookstore, POWERHOUSE Arena, and many others. There are comic book shops and cookbook shops. For most people, especially those who live in car cultures, where they're used to driving to grocery stores and school, it would be nonsensical to think that Brooklyn needed, or could sustain, another independent bookstore. But New York City is different—when BookCourt closed, it

meant that we could no longer just pop into a bookstore with the stroller, that we could no longer walk to a bookstore with our kids. I knew that if that loss felt immense for us, it would feel immense for others, too. We came to the bookstore from an extremely privileged position—my job as a novelist could sustain our family, and we didn't need the bookstore to pay our mortgage. We saw it as a community service, a way to give back something important and vital to both the book community and our neighbors.

I had a few strong feelings: the store needed to feel welcoming to everyone, and comfortable for parents and children, in particular. The store needed to strongly represent women writers, and writers of color. The staff needed to be friendly. There needed to be multiple places to sit down. My husband, who has spent the last two decades as a graphic designer, needed everything to look great, for the actual space to be beautiful.

The 2016 election happened a few weeks into our planning. Like so many people, I needed to be peeled off the floor with a spatula. It was, and remains, a nightmarish heartbreak. That night, and the next morning, we wavered—how could we make such an enormous leap, how could we make a commitment so big, when the world was in tatters? That feeling lasted a few hours, but then the cloud passed, and we realized that the uncertain times, the difficult times, the divisive and scary times, they required safe spaces more than any other. Our bookstore would be a port in the storm.

It's been five months now, as of the moment I'm writing this. Both of my sons are wearing their Books Are Magic (our new shop's name) T-shirts today, just because. (Well, the big one wanted to, and the little one just wants to do whatever the big one does.) The store is wonderfully busy almost every day, and when it's not (like on Monday mornings), we know that the sky is not falling, that it's all part of the routine. We have events almost every night, and a staff of booksellers who are as hilarious and goofy and smart and wonderful as I dreamed. There are hard things—my husband isn't able

There is nowhere I feel more immediately at home and surrounded by friends than at a bookstore.

to come to school pickup as he used to, and I do sometimes feel that we have sacrificed him to the bookstore gods—but I also know that we are still in the newborn period, and that just like with our two babies, the first six months are a blur of breast-feeding and night-wakings, of trying to separate night from day. I know we'll get there eventually.

People find community where they seek it, and where they feel comfortable—playing on a team, or cooking brisket for six hours, or singing in a chorus, or birding, or a million other things—but for me, there is nowhere I feel more immediately at home and surrounded by friends than at a bookstore. Reading and writing are solitary activities, but bookstores aren't solitary places. They aren't even always quiet. They are spilling over with ideas and suggestions and answers, and right now I think we all need all the ideas and suggestions and answers that we can get. If Books Are Magic can offer that, along with a place to sit, and a bathroom with a changing table, and a pink neon sign, well, then I think we're doing okay.

Interview with **Angela Maria Spring,**
founder and owner of **Duende District**

How did you get here, in three sentences or less?
I am a first-generation Latina and my family is from Central America and Puerto Rico. I have been a bookseller in New Mexico, New York City, and Washington, DC, for seventeen years. I had worked with far too few fellow people of color in bookstores, especially in decision-making positions, so I decided to create a bookstore that celebrates and uplifts all voices of color in the book industry to truly serve communities of color, while welcoming everyone to an amazing bookstore experience.

There are so many tasks involved in owning a bookstore—truly, an astonishing number. How do you decide what to delegate to other staff members? Are there things that you assumed you would always do yourself that you are now happy to have others do?

It's still mostly just me, so I've had to learn to do an overwhelming amount of things I'd never done before. However, I have a talented group of POC (people of color) booksellers I've worked with in the past who help create my branding and marketing tools, my website development, and lend their bookselling skills to each individual pop-up space. I have built Duende District as a space for them to shine and they continue to impress me. I am so blessed to have these amazing people on our team.

How important is it to you to have your staff feel a sense of agency?
In my experience as a manager working in large and small bookstore spaces during my career, I firmly believe it is vital for the staff to feel a part of a team and mission, as well as to add their individual strengths to the store. It is a careful balance, but important. As a manager, you should recognize your employees' strengths and weaknesses, help develop their skills, and give them the opportunity to add their individual voice in a meaningful way. That is how you cultivate a positive environment and a sense of agency.

What are your favorite things that you do every day in your bookstore?
It is, always has been, and always will be to be on the book floor, to greet customers, talk to them, then put a book in their hands and tell them why I love it and why I think they'll love it, too.

Now, as the owner/buyer, I get to complete the circle in that every book in Duende District is one I can put in customers' hands confidently. Whatever they choose themselves, I helped put it in their hands. And it's about a thousand percent more meaningful because almost every book I stock is by a person of color.

Who is your customer?
My customer is anyone who believes a bookstore can change our world. My customer is anyone who loves a beautiful, warm, personal bookstore experience. My customer is a person of color who yearns to truly see themselves in their books and bookstores. My customer is anyone who is an ally and champions voices of color. My customer is anyone who knows we must find a way to heal together and changing the narrative through arts and literature is how we can do it.

The publishing world is very white and very male, but there are groups that are shining a light on publishing's prejudices, blind spots, and failings (VIDA, We Need Diverse Books) and also highlighting and celebrating the work of authors of color, and creating vibrant communities (Well-Read Black Girl). What do you do in your store to help forward those goals?

Duende District is by and for people of color—where all are welcome. Almost all of my books are by authors of color. We have POC artist residents in each pop-up and the majority of staff is POC. I truly believe that not only can we create an authentic bookstore experience for communities of color, where they see themselves reflected and celebrated, but also a place where everyone feels invited to be a part of the conversation and experience.

I am a poet and we are taught "show, don't tell." Duende District is all about showing, not telling. It is through our actions that we effect true change. We will sell more books by people of color. We will challenge the publishing industry to produce more books by people of color. We will change what kinds of stories people of color are "allowed" to tell. We will push the industry to hire more editors of color. We will provide a template for other people of color who want to start bookstores in their communities.

In essence, I aim to change the entire book industry, top to bottom, to be more representative. As Angela Davis said, "I am no longer accepting the things I cannot change, I am changing the things I cannot accept."

How much do you actually read? Do you finish everything that you start? Do you designate reading time for the store and reading for pleasure?

My reading habits change with my stress level. I do read two or three books a week, but depending on how stressed-out I am (which is a lot at the moment), the kinds of books change. I mostly read poetry and fiction, with some memoir thrown in.

I don't finish everything I start. I'm also someone who firmly believes if you're reading a book recreationally and are not into it, don't force yourself to finish it. Nothing appalls me more than the idea of disliking something you're reading when you can simply move on to something more to your taste at the moment. Sometimes it isn't the right time in your life to read a particular book. Put it aside, come back to it in a few months or a year later, and it might be the perfect book for you at that time.

What do you think is a bookstore's place in a political climate like ours? Does a bookstore have a responsibility to stay neutral, to stay active, or neither?

Staying neutral is a privilege.

I literally don't get to be neutral. I am a woman of color and first-generation Latinx. My government has basically abandoned my family and people in Puerto Rico with its casual response to an entire island's infrastructure being utterly destroyed by two hurricanes. My government is working to deport thousands of Hispanics who should be citizens, brought here as children by their parents, who were seeking a better life. My government condones white supremacy and racially motivated violence against people of color. My government is targeting Islamic people of color with travel bans.

Bookstore owners should ask themselves—do you get to stay neutral because none of these things personally affects you? Are you afraid you'll offend your customers? Why? What do you think will happen if you take a stance one way or another?

Just getting to ask these questions is a privilege. So I can't say one way or the other whether it's our responsibility or not, but I certainly don't think you're creating a truly open and authentically safe space for any of us who are targeted simply by existing. Being an ally takes courage. Silence is the most dangerous weapon oppression has. It's my fervent hope that my colleagues are courageous leaders who strive to be allies and understand that staying neutral is not a real option.

What are your five-year goals for the store? Ten-year?

I want to open at least one 500- to 800-square-foot store each year, starting in 2018. Each store will be a different model of hybrid business—some partnered within other existing businesses, collectives, or incubating spaces and some stand-alone brick-and-mortar bookstores. The pop-up model lends itself to this model, but I also want to create a flexible business model to suit the needs of each community and to be sustainable in high-rent, high-cost urban areas. This is part of building a new kind of model for bookstores that we can take to people of color all over the country to aid in building their own bookstores.

DUENDE
DISTRICT
POP
UP

→ SEPT 8 → 17

A
CREATIVE DC
BROOKLAND

Interview with **Janet Geddis,**
founder and owner of **Avid Bookshop**

How did you get here, in three sentences or less?
From a very young age, I was obsessed with books.
Though I'd mentioned opening a bookstore as one of my
pipe dreams, I never took it seriously until I found I was
unfulfilled in the various other careers I tried. In 2007, I
announced I was going to open a bookshop in Athens,
Georgia; in 2011, it actually happened.

**There are so many tasks involved in owning a
bookstore—truly, an astonishing number. How do you
decide what to delegate to other staff members? Are
there things that you assumed you would always do
yourself that you are now happy to have others do?**
In my experience, someone who successfully founds her
own business is pretty independent and quite adept at
being in charge. As someone who likes to have at least
relative control over every little thing at Avid Bookshop, I
started delegating only through necessity. I'm chronically
ill (with chronic migraine disease and psoriatic arthritis),
so it was imperative that I have coworkers who can take
care of the day-to-day business so that I diminish my
chances of burnout and sickness. As my business has

grown, I have decided to delegate many tasks, even ones I just love doing. For instance, in late summer 2017 I promoted some longtime booksellers into frontlist (new book) buying roles—even a year ago, I would have told you I'd never give up buying for the shops! I find I have to continually evaluate what parts of the job bring me joy and what parts of the job are not ones I can assign to others, as they're owner-specific. When I get overwhelmed at work, I make myself analyze what is and isn't working at work and in my personal life; essentially, I have to remind myself why I started this business in the first place and the positive impacts I want it to have on all parts of my life. From there, I can decide how I want to redesign my position in order to take care of business while feeling fulfilled.

How important is it to you to have your staff feel a sense of agency?

Giving my staff a sense of agency has grown into one of the most important tenets of my business. While it remains hard to delegate tasks and give coworkers more responsibility, I have seen firsthand how the bookseller and certain aspects of the business really blossom when there's a change in leadership. One challenging thing about being a leader is knowing when to give up parts of your job and allow others to feel ownership over those duties—you have to remind yourself to be okay with the actions taken by the smart, capable people you hired. Most of my managers don't operate the way I would or approach projects the way I do, but their work is excellent—I've had to teach myself to step back and not interfere with the way they run their programs, which can be hard for someone like me!

What are your favorite things that you do every day in your bookstore?

I will never get over the Christmas-morning feeling of opening freshly delivered boxes of books and gifts. It's such an exquisite joy to see what treasures will soon be on the shelves. I also love talking to customers, many of whom have become friends. There are so many people of various ages and backgrounds that I never would've gotten to know were it not for Avid. I'm so grateful.

Who is your customer?

We have all sorts of customers (which means we get to carry all sorts of books!). From the young family taking their toddlers to story time to the teenagers who've been coming to Avid since they were in elementary school to the college students to the professors and retirees, we serve an astonishing variety of readers and couldn't be more thankful for that.

The publishing world is very white and very male, but there are groups that are shining a light on publishing's prejudices, blind spots, and failings (VIDA, We Need Diverse Books) and also highlighting and celebrating the work of authors of color, and creating vibrant communities (Well-Read Black Girl). What do you do in your store to help forward those goals?

Avid Bookshop is proud to be one of the most outspoken businesses we know of when it comes to championing all types of diversity. From the books on the shelves to the displays we make to the events we book to the employees I hire, we aim in all ways to be as welcoming and diverse as possible. During staff meetings, we talk openly about our community's concerns and blind spots, and I encourage my coworkers to take initiative when it comes to what we offer for sale and what programming we book. While we as a business never endorse a political candidate, we are not shy about speaking up for human rights, equality, antidiscrimination, and the fact that we have a long way to go but are willing to learn, listen, and change. We aim to walk the walk and talk the talk, even if it means occasionally becoming a troll's target.

How much does a bookstore reflect its owners' taste and sensibility?

It's been such a pleasure to witness how Avid has evolved over the years. I see my influence most significantly in the way we present ourselves to the world: we are unabashedly enthusiastic about books we love, and we completely adore our town and our customers. By the same token, I have decided to be open and honest about our struggles, from dealing with crappy weekend sales over a football game weekend to the impact chronic illness has on our ability to do all the things we aim to do. As the business has grown over the years, I've not only allowed but encouraged my booksellers to let their personalities shine through; six years after opening Avid Bookshop on Prince Avenue, I'm proud to see how funky and welcoming my business is, thanks to the truly kind people I work with.

How much do you actually read? Do you finish everything that you start? Do you designate reading time for the store and reading for pleasure?

Though I occasionally deal with reading ruts, I tend to read at least fifty books a year, not including picture books (which I read frequently!). I've become less precious with my reading habits since starting my business—if I start a book, especially an advanced copy of something—I will put it down if it's not doing anything for me.

What do you think is a bookstore's place in a political climate like ours? Does a bookstore have a responsibility to stay neutral, to stay active, or neither?

I feel very strongly that Avid's prominent position in Athens and in the literary community at large bestows upon us the responsibility to be a voice for people who need one. We are fervent supporters of equality, a healthy environment, science, justice, and open-mindedness. I find it utterly heartbreaking that taking a stand for human rights is seen as a political move, one to be attacked by those who want to aid the oppressors. We have gotten more outspoken as the days have passed, and I anticipate many more heartbreaking conversations with staff about what we will do next to let our community know we are a safe, welcoming place.

How much do your stores' neighborhood/city have to do with its personality?

My bookshops (I have two) are definitely neighborhood-focused. While they're only two miles apart, they both reflect their individual neighborhoods very well. Athens is a fascinating creative enclave, where literally every other person is a musician, artist, writer, poet, or all of the above. Athens is eclectic and joyful and progressive and smart, and I believe my bookshops reflect that.

What are your five-year goals for the store? Ten-year?

I want Avid to flourish so that we can continue to provide gainful employment to the twenty-plus people who work here. Businesswise, I constantly seek ways to improve our profit margin (note to non-bookstore people: this business is notorious for its lack of profit), increase the quality of life for my staff and community, and solidify systems that will keep us successful for the long haul. In ten years' time, I want to look back and feel proud of the work I've done and the voices I've helped to empower.

Every day, people come in to the store and ask if we'll sell their small press or self-published books and magazines. That sale is up to the taste of the buyer, and how they feel their customer will connect with your book. Don't take it personally! Unless you live around the corner and will send all of your family members to the bookstore and are in there shopping every single day, the bookstore is under no obligation to carry copies of anyone's book. There is limited space in every bookstore, even big ones, and it's important not to take their decision personally.

WHAT TO DO

1 If you live near an independent bookstore, go visit them. Ask the booksellers who does the buying. They will likely give you an email address. Write an email to that person with information about your book. What they will probably tell you is to drop off or send over a copy for them to look at—you will not get that copy back. If their office is anything like mine, the buyer is sitting in a sea of books all the time, and you don't want to give them more to do.

2 If you want your book in other bookstores, ones that are not near enough to visit, just send a copy to the attention of the store's buyer with a note saying why you think the book would be a good fit for the store.

3 Follow up, once or maybe twice. Just check in. Everyone is busy.

4 It helps to have your own platform—whether that's a great social media presence, a website, or some other thing to point buyers to. They want to be able to distinguish your book from the hundreds of other books sitting in piles around their desk. Don't be afraid to be goofy, or, at the very least, to do something that makes it clear that you are not a robot. The buyer is not a robot either, and if they can separate you from the pack of form letters, they will be much more likely to want to carry your book.

WHAT NOT TO DO

1 Do not call multiple times (or ask your loved ones to call multiple times, pretending not to be the author). I did this. This will not endear you to the booksellers.

2 Don't worry too much about the print quality—the buyer understands that this is just a sample. If it's an art book, though, the quality is important, so make sure whatever you send communicates how the finished product will look. If you feel like your finished copy is too expensive to send to lots of places, ask if you can send a digital copy. People will like that. Less waste for all involved.

3 That's really it. Some stores are very open to carrying zines and small magazines and have a great system in place, and some stores don't. It never hurts to try. Good luck!

Why is it important to talk openly about mental health?

by Kat Kinsman

illustrations by Avery Kua

Mental illness can make us feel we are less than human, keep us from caring for ourselves, and isolate us for fear of what others might think. I asked four extraordinary writers—Beejoli Shah, Ashley C. Ford, Parker Molloy, and Esmé Weijun Wang—about their decision to stand up against the stigma and speak openly about their own experiences.

ASHLEY: People don't always understand mental illness and might stereotype you, but I'm a black queer woman, so I'm used to being stereotyped. I don't allow that ignorance to steal my joy. The reward of talking about it openly has been more honest conversations with every person in my life.

PARKER: It's easy to discount someone you can label as being "crazy." But the biggest reward—being able to be your authentic self and not have to hide something that's a part of you—is worth it.

BEEJOLI: You may risk that someone will use the information you've disclosed as a way to categorize you—to line up all your sins as proof that you cannot be trusted, and use your diagnosis as proof that they are right to line up said sins. The proof in the pudding is that you are crazy, basically, beyond repair. But the reward is that is rarely the case. And when it is, it's easy to see whom to move out of your life.

ESMÉ: I sometimes feel what's been called a "vulnerability hangover" because of speaking so openly. But I keep doing it, and I think it's a good thing to do.

What is your official diagnosis/condition, and what are the words you personally use to describe it?

ASHLEY: I am a person who lives with depression, generalized anxiety, and PTSD.

PARKER: Major depressive disorder, panic/anxiety disorders.

BEEJOLI: Generalized anxiety disorder and depression.

ESMÉ: Schizoaffective disorder, bipolar type, generalized anxiety disorder, and C-PTSD (complex post-traumatic stress disorder).

What made you decide to publicly speak about your mental health?

ASHLEY: Once I found spaces with many people who shared different aspects of their lives online, I realized I wasn't alone. I felt affirmed and liberated by them. So much of the peace I was beginning to find with myself came from other people choosing to share their words and experiences. I wanted to pay it forward.

PARKER: I was sick of hating myself. I was sick of always being sad or angry or upset or just feeling broken because I tried to bottle so much of this up.

ESMÉ: One, I was hired full-time at a start-up company. Two, I realized that if I didn't speak publicly about it then, there was no better time waiting in the wings for me. Being hired full-time was important because I'd previously worried that talking about mental illness would make me unhirable.

What was the impact on your life from your disclosure?

PARKER: There were some messages of encouragement, there were some angry trolls online who took advantage of that new information. In all, it was easier, at least compared to some of the other things I've had to "come out" as: being trans, being bisexual.

BEEJOLI: I was more honest with myself right away. Instead of rationalizing my behaviors (lying to people I cared about over small things; picking fights constantly; never standing up for myself and then boiling over), I was able to recognize them and with the help of meds, able to manage my reactions to them without instantly going from 0 to 120.

Why are stigma and silence so dangerous?

ESMÉ: I received, and still do receive, a lot of emails from people, particularly young women, who were and are relieved to see me speaking publicly about living with mental illness.

BEEJOLI: The relief at finding out that you're not a bad person, you're just a person, is the very, very best, and I wouldn't want anyone to deny themselves that.

ESMÉ: Stigma and silence keep people from seeking help. People die from stigma and silence.

Are there different risks for POC, LGBTQ+, or people from certain religious or cultural backgrounds in discussing mental health?

ASHLEY: I've been told black people don't get to be crazy. I've been asked, "Isn't being queer enough?" And I've been encouraged to just pray it away. It's all so wrong, but I have to be strong enough in my own mind to know they're wrong. I feel terribly for all the people still struggling with these bad beliefs and ideas.

BEEJOLI: Exclusion from the community. Parental exclusion. I've been lucky that my community has been for the most part ultra supportive, but it still does bug me when that uncle (whom I love and am super close to), or people like him, use my diagnosis to make judgments about my life.

ESMÉ: Mental health issues can be an invisible marginal identifier, though not always, and it might be risky to exhibit that and make it plain.

How would you advise someone to disclose their mental health issues?

ASHLEY: Tell the people you *need* to tell first. At least one person who will definitely have your back, and at least one person whom you trust to help you when you need it.

PARKER: Depending on what the issue is, talk to your therapist/doctor/whatever you have beforehand.

ESMÉ: There's a saying from Danielle LaPorte that I think about often: "Open heart. Big fucking fence." Not everyone is going to respond well. Be aware of that going in.

How can people support someone in their life who opens up about their mental health?

ASHLEY: Listen without judgment, encourage without shaming, and love fiercely before anything else.

PARKER: Listen. Do your homework. Make yourself available.

BEEJOLI: Just be there. Listen. *Don't* weigh in with "Hey, do you need to see your therapist again?" or "Do you need to adjust your meds?" Do be a support, but don't be an armchair therapist.

STRENGTH ON AND OFF THE STAGE

by Grace Bonney

photographs by
Sasha Israel

When Cynthia Erivo walks into a room, all eyes are on her. She exudes the sort of bravery, courage, and confidence that's needed to perform in front of hundreds of people, as she does on a regular basis. In her career as a Grammy, Emmy and Tony Award–winning singer and actress, Cynthia has performed on countless stages, from Broadway to the Kennedy Center.

But Cynthia doesn't require a huge stage to give her all. Sometimes a busy Manhattan gym is the space where she shines and inspires those around her to achieve their own version of greatness. In regular videos, uploaded to her Instagram account, Cynthia shared her daily physical challenges in the form of powerful pull-ups, acrobatic backbends, and feats of strength that can only be described as awe-inspiring.

Cynthia is a regular at Dogpound, a gym in New York City where we met to talk about the ways physical health and fitness have impacted her life and work. Watching her catch up with trainers and friends in the gym, I saw that her devotion to hard work (and inspiring others) isn't limited to performance time. It's also clear that she's found a home in this space where she can have support and encouragement from people who share her commitment to health and wellness.

It's in gyms like this that Cynthia has worked so hard to build a body that allows her to do as many of the things she loves as possible. Her drive toward fitness helps her have the stamina to do everything from performing in multiple Broadway shows per day to using her voice to speak up for social justice and political causes she believes in.

We sat down after her workout session to talk about how she found her voice, embraced the power of her body, and learned to reclaim her space with pride and inspire others to the do same.

How and when did fitness become such a huge part of your life?

I started to realize that I could be physically fit when I was about eleven, and I hated it. I used to get made fun of because I had stronger arms, and that was different from most girls. But later on that year, I realized that I could do the same things that the boys could do and I relished in that. Then I started to take advantage of my strength and really enjoyed being physical. The more I noticed what a benefit it was to me, the more I wanted to feel it.

How does fitness impact and affect your life and work now?

I was twenty-one when I did my first big musical and realized that my fitness was what allowed me to do the thing I loved. I was performing onstage eight days a week, and relaxing in my off time wasn't helping me keep up with that schedule. Being physical and getting my body in shape to be onstage helped me do more of what I loved.

When you discover what I call your "power substance," which for me is working out, you just keep going with it. I also realized how many people were encouraged by someone like me—a small, young woman—doing all this physical activity. So I wanted to show that it's okay to be strong—and look strong.

I may go slightly overboard sometimes [Cynthia famously ran a half-marathon and performed in back-

Being physical and getting my body in shape to be on stage helped me do more of what I loved.

to-back Broadway performances in one day], but I do all these physical things because it's how I separate myself from who I am on the stage. It's a healthy way of saying, "This is Cynthia. This is the time and space she needs. And then this is the character. This is the character's space." It's a way for me to separate the two.

What's the difference between how you feel when you walk in the gym and when you walk out?
I'm always really excited to get to the gym. Along the way, I've picked up people who are in my life constantly now, just because I've met them at the gym and spent so much time with them. Once I'm in the gym, I'm always super focused. Everything comes into one center. When I finish, I always feel like I achieved something, and that feels good. It's never easy at the gym. But give me a challenge, and I'll work toward bettering myself.

Gym culture can be intimidating. How did you find a way to make gyms feel like a safe space for you?
When I go into the gym, I bring an energy of togetherness and happiness. I go to the gym to meet people and say hello. I know people who are just beginning might feel intimidated, so I always try to find a way to communicate with that person, just to say, "You're doing really well! We can all be at different stages, but we're all working very hard." I always try to make sure I've met everyone and spoken to everyone, so that it's always fun when we get together.

How do you maintain your commitment to physical health when you're on the road?
When I'm traveling, I just work out in my hotel room. I'll call my trainer, Kirk, on FaceTime and we'll just get to work.

I always make sure I have enough space wherever I'm staying so that there's no excuse to not work out. I have workout equipment (like bands) that folds up and can fit in my suitcase—and away I go!

You were in an all-female production of *Henry IV* where you played the Earl of Douglas and said you enjoyed being able to take up space without being asked to be smaller or quieter. You seem to have really learned to relish your voice and owning your space with pride. What was your journey to that self-acceptance and love?
I think I just realized that each person has their own unique qualities. And I like who I am. I don't believe that it serves me or anyone else to cut that in half, or to take away bits and pieces, and only serve you a small amount of it. Who does that serve? It makes me feel uncomfortable, and I think it makes another person feel uncomfortable.

If a person is uncomfortable with me as a whole, then that's not my problem. I can't do anything about that. I think that it's important as women to become certain in who you are, so that when you do present yourself, you're not having to lessen what you have. You shouldn't have to compartmentalize certain bits of yourself so someone else will feel better about you.

I don't feel like it's ever served me to be anything less than everything I am. I don't really know how to do anything other than take up the space that I'm in. It's just how I'm built. I can't apologize for the strange things that I am, because they're so much a part of me that that's just it. I'm never not going to be muscular. That's just how I am. That's how my body is. I've done so much for it that it's always going to be that way. I'm never not going to have a gap between my teeth, because that's the way I was born. I'm never not going to be able to have a big smile, because that's just how it is. Those things that make me me are the things that I have to just enjoy and go forward.

Do you remember what it felt like the first time you stepped out on a stage? And did it make you feel vulnerable?

The first professional role where I felt like I was vulnerable and just myself was a play I did right after RADA (the Royal Academy of Dramatic Art). It was Marine Parade and I was playing a fourteen-year-old. There had to be an innocence to the character and in order to do that, I had to let everything go and just *be* there, present. It is scary to just be there; whatever happens, happens. People are watching you and you just have to go with it. Now I find that feeling thrilling, because you really don't know what's going to happen. You know that you have words to say. You know that you have to get from A to B. How that happens really depends on what the other person gives you and what you want to give to them. Then, the rest is history.

It was a little daunting when I first discovered that that's what I needed to do in order to access the places in my performance that I wanted to. It can be scary for people to be honest. You have to take away all the stuff and make it about just yourself and the words and the music, and just tell the truth. Some people feel that to be onstage and to act is to be presentational. But actually, it isn't that at all. It's just to bring the story to someone as truthfully as you possibly can. That might be really messy. That might be really painful. That might be really daunting, but that's actually what people are paying for. I just sort of came to grips with it and dove in and did that.

With that deep vulnerability you bring to the stage, how do you protect yourself in your real life? What does your support system look like?

I have a group of friends whom I go to when I need help. I have older women whom I call and I think that's important. I think everyone needs to have their mentors

You are allowed to walk into a space and be yourself wholly. You can be successful and being yourself can work.

and their pillars that they go to when everything feels out of whack. You need those people who are close to you, like your colleagues and your friends and your peers, who understand what's happening. Those are the people you can go to if you need a bit of support and lifting.

I do set up boundaries for myself, though. There are things that I don't tolerate ever. I don't like lies. Lying doesn't suit or serve me. If I feel like I'm talking to someone who isn't being honest, that gets cut off automatically. I don't have the wherewithal to deal with that.

I also make sure that I live holistically. I don't drink. I don't smoke. I don't do drugs. I eat specifically (I'm vegan). All of that aids my health and is my sort of protection, for my body and my heart.

How do you bring that energy into auditions when you are trying to embody someone else?

I decided that I would go as me, 100 percent of the time. It's the only thing that I feel has really gotten me where I am. I don't know how to be anything other than me. I got tired of hearing that people have to be something else. I just didn't want that to be how I became what I am, or what I could become. I want to be able to confidently say to people. "You are allowed to walk into a space and be yourself wholly. You can be successful and being yourself can work."

How do you edit and nurture that support system so that it's honest and real?

I set up disclaimers when I first meet people. If I feel that we're about to become good friends, I will let you know that I'm honest and expect the same.

That goes for my team at work, too. They know that I don't need frills, I just need the truth. I might not always like it, but I appreciate it. It helps me know where I really am.

We are in a time where honesty and truth are our strongest instruments. We really need to use them more. We need to make sure that people know that they don't have to say yes all the time. Nobody needs a yes all the time, because you can't grow from that.

You bring this honesty and directness to social media as well. How do you handle some of the challenging conversations that can happen there?

One of my stipulations for any answer to anyone is to never call anyone out by name. I never call people names. I never swear at people, ever. I don't believe that's constructive. I don't believe that's helpful. I tend to go strictly for facts—and things I know about. I speak up about things I believe are truthful and right. I always think that if it's a teachable moment, then that's what I'm going to be doing.

So many young actresses look up to you and want to be "the next Cynthia Erivo." But you always encourage them to be themselves first. How do you do that and why is that so important to you?

I often hear "I want to be Cynthia. I want to be you." But in those moments I know that in order to be me, you would have to know the things that I've been through. Those things that I've been through might not be the things you have to go through. I would rather you embrace the person you are and nurture that. That might be better than I am. Why would you take away a chance for yourself to be better than something? We don't need three hundred Cynthias. We need three hundred individual, different people. That means there's variation and difference and beauty. That's why I keep encouraging young people to really zone in on what they want, what they need.

I feel like people are afraid of asking for success—especially young people. What do you want? Do you want to win an Oscar at some point in your life? Yes? That's okay. You can say that. Do you want to be a Nobel Peace Prize winner? Yes? That's okay, too. You can say that. You have to tease it out of people, because somewhere along the line, we're told that we're not allowed to expect the greatest from ourselves. How can we pursue that if we don't ask for it, or talk about it, or speak on it?

I feel like when you put something out, you give the universe its beginning. You tell the universe, "I'm ready for this, so let's start working for it."

What are the characteristics or attributes that the women in your support system, and the women you look up to, have in common?

I tend to draw people who are superconfident in everything they are. One of my friends, Luvvie Ajayi, is confident in exactly who and what she is. She's the girl who loves a blazer and a fedora and flat shoes and has no qualms about it. We were talking about going to Oprah's Super Soul Sunday brunch and the first thing she said was, "I need to get a new blazer and I need a fedora." I was like, "I knew you were going to wear that, because that's what you wear. That's you."

A lot of the women whom I know and are dear to me happen to be African women. We all know what it is to be African women out of Africa, but still very much within Africa with our families. We all are striving for excellence. We all want the best from ourselves. We all have the hardest asks of ourselves. We don't shy away from that. We have all experienced troubles that have been harder to deal with on our own, and have no hesitations about reaching out and saying, "Hey, do you need a hand?" We have no problems with taking a break. We say, "Step back for a minute, take a moment, breathe, and we'll get back to it."

We are a real support system. I think that's sort of what draws us together, because those similarities are the things that make us strong as human beings. When you put us together, we're undefeatable.

I like who I am.
I don't believe
that it serves me
or anyone else to
cut that in half.

HOW I FOUND MY WAY TO ARTIVISM

By: Miriam Klein Stahl

In my first week after moving to San Francisco in 1989 I saw an ACT UP (AIDS COALITION TO UNLEASH POWER) "Die-In". Hundreds of people were lying down in the street while others outlined their bodies in chalk to leave an impression of all the people dying of AIDS as the government turned its back.

That same week I went to hear Emory Douglas, minister of information for the Black Panther Party give an artist talk and slide show at a Brazilian restaraunt. He called himself a movement artist and talked about making images that people in the community could identify with. He said he doesn't make art because it is fun (though it is), but because it is needed to educate and elevate community. Those early experiences paved the way for me to become an artivist.

In 1995, I became a public school art teacher.

In my capacity as a teacher I work with teenagers to discover the use of art as a powerful political and cultural tool that is also a means of individual and collective expression.

RAD WOMEN

In 2014 my friend Kate Schatz approached me about illustrating an A-Z kids book about radical American women. She sent me a five page email asking me to collaborate. I answered with one word "YES". Kate and I are about to release our third book together, Rad Girls Can in the summer of 2018. The success of the books speak to the need for women to be seen as vibrant makers of our global arts, science, politics and culture.

The time is NOW!

In the summer of 2017 the Mayor of Berkeley approached me and My wife, artist Lena Wolff to design a poster to articulate our beliefs as a city after several hateful rallies took place in our community. Lena and I had been hosting Solidarity Sunday meetings at our house since the 2016 presidential election when people in our community felt a need to activate and participate in politics. We take action on relevant timely issues by making phone calls, writing letters to our elected officials and having small group discussions over a community potluck. At one of our meetings with the help of former student and graphic designer Lexi Visco, we made a singular poster that reads BERKELEY STANDS UNITED AGAINST HATE Now over 50,000 of these posters have been adapted and printed for cities all over the Bay Area and they're visible in windows and homes all around town. By doing this, we feel less isolated in our activism and together we bolster each other up.

BERKELEY STANDS UNITED AGAINST HATE

GET UP AND GO MAKE

THE RIPPLE

EFFECT

Designer Dawn Hancock talks with three business owners about the intersection of activism, creativity, and business.

by Dawn Hancock

have no business owning a business. I never took a single business class. And I never even considered writing a business plan. But for some reason, when asked where I saw myself in five years during my first interview out of college, I blurted out, "I want to run my own studio!"

First of all: don't ever say that in an interview. Nobody wants to invest in someone when they know they're going to leave soon. About a year into my first job, they found out I had been looking for my next step and fired me on the spot.

But I was lucky. My work was decent, and I came up in the mid-'90s, a time when there were more jobs than designers. While I was years away from embracing my inner entrepreneur, it was during this time that I started volunteering at a number of nonprofits in town and found a new job at a big, corporate tech firm. Over the two years I worked there, I gained a lot of practical experience, but more important, I learned that I wasn't interested in working on huge corporate websites. Then my dad died unexpectedly. And my entire life was turned upside down.

At the age of twenty-four, I was officially an orphan. I watched my mom die from lung cancer when I was ten, so the death of my father underlined what I already knew but had not yet felt compelled to act on—life is short, so you better make the best of it. And that's when I decided to take the leap and start my own studio.

I had no idea what I was doing. But what I did know was that I wanted to do work that I believed in and that made a difference in people's lives.

I focused on working for nonprofits and small businesses. I could

Dawn Hancock

see how all those volunteer projects I had designed over the past couple years really made a difference for those organizations.

That was almost twenty years ago, and today I manage an eighteen-person studio called Firebelly Design. We've evolved over the years, but we never wavered in our pledge to work with people we respect who are making our world a better place.

Community has always played a pivotal role in Firebelly's work and culture. From our nonprofit that teaches life skills to underserved families in our neighborhood to our annual type-based art show, we've infused giving back to our various communities in everything we do.

In addition to working with organizations that are supporting our local community, Firebelly Design runs programs that make that type of giving back a permanent part of our mission.

Reasons to Give, our education program, was born out of the 2008 financial crash. Increased gentrification was pushing African American and Puerto Rican families, who have been in our community for generations, out of the area and we wanted to find a way to support them.

I started talking to local organizations to find out what we could do. We learned that basic needs were not being met. I knew I didn't have the money to make a significant impact alone, but I did have an office full of people willing to put in the hard work. Our goal was simple: to help the individuals in my neighborhood using our network and a brand-new digital tool my team would build.

While we started as a platform for basic needs, we quickly began offering classes around topics our participants were seeking. Today the model is completely education-focused with specific drives for specialty items throughout the year.

One of the best pieces of advice my dear friend and mentor Rick Valicenti gave me very early on was "It's not business, it's personal." I didn't realize it at the time, but that mantra was my natural instinct and we've been doing it all along.

There are few things better than being a part of someone's growth. Seeing them use the skills and opportunities you've helped provide and find the confidence they had hiding inside the whole time. And hopefully, if you've really made an impact, the torch will have been passed and the process will start all over again.

I reached out to three more entrepreneurs using their skills and talents to run businesses that give back and support their communities. We talked about how their businesses came to be and what role giving back plays in their business model and long-term plans.

Creative Reaction Lab

A design studio for young people dedicated to inclusive and equitable solutions.

What is the mission of your organization?

Creative Reaction Lab educates, trains, and challenges cities to co-create solutions with black and Latinx populations to design healthy and racially equitable communities.

By 2040, blacks and Latinx individuals will make up almost 40 percent of the United States population, and yet these populations face disproportionate racial inequities, limiting social, economic, and cultural growth. Disparities are built into communities through systems of policy, education, housing, criminal justice, etc. We want to work to undo that and create more equity within these communities.

How did you find yourself doing this work? What was your path here?

Early in my career, I focused on the recruitment and retention of racially diverse individuals with the sectors of higher education, advertising, arts administration, and design. This background led to my position as head of communications at Diversity Awareness Partnership. It was within this role that I extended my work from pipeline development to designing inclusive and equitable systems. Due to this, I started to focus on improving people's life expectancy and cultural appreciation/acceptance.

Antionette Carroll

Fast-forward to 2014, and I began to transition from a 9-to-5 graphic designer to a social entrepreneur and community designer. As a former resident of Ferguson, I found that Michael Brown Jr.'s death amplified my frustrations regarding systemic racism and the lack of community voice when responding to civic issues. With the consequences of systemic oppression and the lack of community input rearing its head through riots and city division, I saw the need for a space of inclusion, creativity, action. Therefore, I created Creative Reaction Lab.

Why is it important to you personally?

Recognizing the day-to-day effects of racial inequity in the United States and the minimizing and/or erasure of marginalized community voices wasn't just a job but a personal calling. I've lived the effects of racial inequity, including being raised in poverty by my grandparents and, during college, being obligated to temporarily raise my four siblings because my mother was incarcerated. I acknowledge that my experiences are not unique, especially for black and brown people. This reality drives me.

What's the best advice you've been given since starting?

You can only get so far with you. However, with a community, your possibilities are endless.

The notion of community is unique for everyone, how do you experience it in your life?

Community is everywhere. My family is a community. My workplace is a community. And, of course, our neighborhoods are communities. Communities are made up of people, not buildings. That understanding drives my work at Creative Reaction Lab and as a community leader. "Community members" (also known as living experts) are everywhere and have the opportunity to transform from within any situation. Therefore, I see communities as systems of transformation.

How has giving back to the community played a role in the work you are doing?

Being an active citizen or member of a community is more than voting or volunteerism. To me, civic engagement is addressing issues of public concern using the talent, skills, and expertise one has to make a difference. My personal mission in life is to *challenge* standards, make *change*, and *champion* approaches resulting in systemic and community impact, and I'm inspired by others who, like me, challenge the status quo of oppression and inequities.

I'm giving back through many community-based committees and boards, including being on St. Louis City's Resiliency Steering Committee. I'm also the founding chair of the diversity and inclusion task for AIGA. As the founding chair of the task force, I created an in-house Diversity and Inclusion Task Force, conducted the first staff diversity training in AIGA's 102-year history, restarted the Design Journeys archive highlighting prominent designers of color throughout design history, co-developed the international Design Census, in partnership with Google, and more. Lastly, I'm the co-founder and co-host of the Design + Diversity Conference and Podcast. Honestly, community-based work is my work.

What has been your greatest accomplishment to date?
Systems of oppression, inequalities, and inequities are by design. Therefore, only intentional design can dismantle them. While founding Creative Reaction Lab was, and continues to be, a feat in itself, my greatest accomplishment to date was developing a new framework with the ability to transform the design and diversity, equity, and inclusion industries. To develop creatively talented community members into creatively talented leaders, I've pioneered a new form of creative problem-solving called Equity-Centered Community Design. Equity-Centered Community Design is a unique creative problem-solving process based on equity, humility-building, integrating holistic history and acknowledging trauma due to oppression, addressing power dynamics, and co-creating with community members. After being a practicing designer for ten years and trainer for three, I realized that while design thinking and human-centered design are great tools for institutional problem-solving and consulting, they were not the best approach when addressing complex inequities, violations of human rights, and social injustices. Therefore, I developed a process that put equity and people first.

What's next for you and your organization?
The demand for Creative Reaction Lab's new Design to Better Our Community program and Equity-Centered Community Design process have heavily increased. To date, we've received requests from almost a dozen community members and institutions in cities regarding the scaling of the program—even before the launch of our full summer academy in St. Louis and Chicago during the summer of 2018. Currently, we're focusing on building capacity (and processes) to meet scaling demand.

I'm also traveling to two cities a week to train community members on the Equity-Centered

Community Design process. I hope to develop an education system that will develop the creative capacity of those working on equity challenges through trainings, content focused on thought leadership, online community building, etc. The development of this tool is in the future.

What impact do you hope to have in your community in ten years?
My goal is to have thousands of equity-centered community designers transform our current institutions, particularly the education, media, government and public service, and health and healthcare sectors.

My personal mission in life is to *challenge* standards and make *change*.

Drive Change

A food truck workplace for returning citizens.

What is the mission of your organization?

We are tapping into the talent of young New Yorkers. We use our food truck and catering/hospitality business to run a paid-premiere fellowship for returning citizens (ages eighteen to twenty-five).

How did you find yourself doing this work? What was your path here?

I was a teacher at the public high school on Rikers Island for three years. New York is one of only two states that sets the age of adult criminality at just sixteen years old. Therefore, if you are arrested at sixteen and incarcerated, you will go to an adult facility.

My young students possessed tremendous talent, but the road ahead of them was paved with red lights in the form of barriers to their employment, education, and even their ability to return home if they lived in public housing. One of the only areas of humanity, connection, discipline, real education, teamwork, and pride inside Rikers Island was in a culinary arts class.

Jordyn Lexton

In this setting, students were able to practice the therapeutic nature of cooking and the restorative action of serving food you've made to someone else. In a place that constantly works to break down your sense of self and dehumanize your core being, the kitchen/culinary class was a place where people built each other up.

Then during one of my English classes, a student asked if he could be an architect one day. I concluded, after a lengthy response about hard work, going back to school, and his knack for mathematics, "Yes, I do think you can be an architect."

A student who had been asleep for the entire first half of the discussion raised his head and yelled, "Oh *hell no!*" He said, "No disrespect, I appreciate what you are doing here, but you are selling dreams."

And in that moment my ideology about the injustice of the system and my practical brain collided and I realized that if we were not active in broadening access to opportunity for young adults coming out of the system—I would be forever selling dreams.

So, I thought, what if a food truck business could be a platform for employment and learning? We could use the operations of the business to teach industry-specific and social/emotional skills and we could use the power of hospitality/food as a tool for building community and raising awareness about injustice inside of the system. How do we make a concept like that more active? We don't just start a brick-and-mortar and let people come to us, we put the idea on wheels and bring it to them.

Why is it important to you personally?

I grew up on the Upper East Side of Manhattan and attended a very privileged private school. I lived in a world where doors were always open to me. I was networking before I knew what networking was. For me, the road ahead was paved with all green lights.

The stark contrast between my access to opportunity and the access that my students on Rikers Island had is personal—it is clear to me that environmental conditions and support networks are what make or break someone's genius. Drive Change cannot fully address the trauma that young adults in our criminal justice system face; we cannot (alone) undo the working of white supremacy and structural racism— but we can work to raise awareness and question our presumed norms, which are steeped in capitalism, power, and control.

What's the best advice you've been given since starting?

Learn how to get out of your own way. Delegate, delegate, delegate.

The notion of community is unique for everyone. How do you experience it in your life?

It's through food and sports. That has always been my truth. As a gender-queer trans-masculine person who grew up playing women's sports, I found myself when I was on the field, when my full physicality/strength and extra testosterone were additives and I felt fully connected with my purpose.

I live in Brooklyn with my partner, Dani. We cook for people, it's what we do—it's how we show love. At the table, with my partner, my family, my friends—it is through cooking and sharing meals that community deepens for me.

How has giving back to the community played a role in the work you are doing?

Drive Change is not a charity. It feels more like a movement, or a part of a larger movement. It's a commitment to reimagine things differently. To ask the what-if questions: What if workplaces were designed to be healing? What if nonprofits could be cooperative structures? What if the criminal justice system was not confined by our ideas of crime and punishment? What if workplaces were designed to be a tool for learning? What if hospitality built community and restored trust? What if white people weren't in control?

Asking these questions alongside the young people we employ at Drive Change and building the community around them so they can harness their own genius also puts them in the driver seat to be change agents themselves. This ability to have the voice of young adults impacted directly by the system thinking concretely about alternatives and workplace practices grounded in love is as profound for me as I believe it is for them.

Have you had any conflicts or challenges choosing to have a social impact mission over a traditional bottom-line-driven approach?

Yeah! We're an underfunded start-up hybrid (a nonprofit that wholly owns a for-profit subsidiary), and we're committed to working with people who are very new to work. That means we have to be very clear about what our expectations are and have infrastructure in place to help support learning while doing (while being in a competitive food market!). Oh, and we are designed to turn staff over every year (our fellowship is one year

long), so we have to deal with training gaps. Over time, these operational challenges have gotten better because we've been able to practice different solutions, but when you're first building something and things are flying at you left and right, you're bound to get some things wrong.

I think our steadfastness, met with the substance of what we do, is helping to develop the idea of a "Food Business for Social Justice" and gets other business owners and managers into the notion that they, too, can use their own operations as tools for building up their teams.

I believe people are becoming more socially conscious consumers, and we definitely see that our mission helps us get events/gigs much more than it ever hurts us.

What has been your greatest accomplishment to date?

Our food truck won the Vendy Award for best food truck in New York City in 2015—that was amazing. It was like winning the championship alongside all of these incredible people who had committed themselves deeply to what

we are about. That moment was a total validation of our business and our team. We've also secured incredible opportunities like becoming an Echoing Green fellow, and being able to tap into the immense talent of people in the social enterprise space throughout the world.

What's next for you and your organization?

Drive Change 2.0, baby! We're pumped about the future. We are looking ahead to the idea that hospitality can (and should) be a tool for social justice.

First, we're expanding our catering and events operation so we can hire even more young people coming home from jail/prison. We redesigned our food truck this summer and the vibe/brand is very in-line with the Drive Change mission.

Rather than build more food businesses ourselves as a platform for growth (a costly and operationally complex way to scale), we are going to tap into the strength of other like-minded food businesses that are reaching out to us and asking to hire our fellows. Our next chapter is an affiliation model where other food businesses can apply to become Drive Change–certified.

We are moving into an affiliation model because we have seen the demand from other small food businesses to affiliate with Drive Change so they can hire from our talent pool of returning citizens and receive coaching services from our team about how to use their own management/operations to build the social/emotional growth of their staff.

We are taking this two-prong approach to workplace development: an idea that not only do potential employees need to be incubated, but managers/owners need to be trained as well and hold themselves accountable to provide working conditions that build their teams up rather than break their teams down.

We're pumped to do this in the food/hospitality space because we think it's an industry that is really well suited for this work.

Project H Design

An architecture program that connects young people with their community.

What is the mission of your organization?

Project H Design exists as a nonprofit to give young people the space and voice to build physical change in their communities. We do that in a number of different ways (within the high school classroom, after school, over the summer, and by supporting other teachers), but the mission and ongoing question is always the same: how can we give young people the tools to build (literally!) a tangible change in their own lives and neighborhoods?

I think in public education we often dilute real-world experiences to the "kid version" of adult work. But we believe that teenagers can build a farmer's market to transform their town, and that that structure can end up in *Architectural Record,* and that those kids can see a different future and career and become the authors of their own lives. We know that because we've done it.

One aspect of our mission is to ask that exact question—who gets to make our world (and who doesn't)?—then to work to change the authorship of our physical world. Why shouldn't makers be young people, or young girls of color, or anyone who has ever been underestimated or marginalized by their communities? We fundamentally believe in the power of design and brick-and-mortar building to open up the universe for kids. Especially for young girls through our program Girls Garage, we want to create the space and conditions for total badass hands-on work that breaks down any doubt or barriers.

How did you find yourself doing this work? What was your path here?

This all started from a place of frustration in my own architectural career. If I rewind to my teenage days, I was very lucky to discover architecture and building as a way of understanding the world, that creating space was a way of bringing people together, building beauty, and having a

Emily Pilloton

real impact. After my junior year of high school, I worked in Belize for the summer learning how to pour concrete, cut rebar, frame walls, and build a gazebo and community center in a small town there. That experience solidified for me the importance of not just community-based architecture, but also the value of hands-on work, actually doing the concrete-mixing and wall-raising yourself. I studied architecture at UC Berkeley and the School of the Art Institute and began working in the fields of architecture and design after graduation.

What I discovered within the "industry" of architecture and design was that many of the things I loved most about building (community, hands-on work, etc.) were far removed from the architectural office. I also discovered I do not deal with authority well and hated working for a boss, on someone else's ideas. So in 2008, I quit working for other people and in the "industry," and started Project H as a nonprofit.

Why is it important to you personally?

I feel very lucky to have had a few key experiences as a young person that helped me move throughout the world with confidence and optimism. This work is so important to me because I feel that every kid deserves that, yet far from every kid gets those moments. For some young people, those moments might be because of a teacher who believes in them, or a parent, or an internship, or an important friendship. For me, as a young girl, and a mixed-race young woman growing up in a nearly all-white community, I experienced these "aha" moments when I had my hands in the dirt and then could step back and point to something and say, "I built that." Nothing else in my entire life has given me such confidence and belief in the power of human beings to do good than building something that did not exist before, and especially something that could benefit others.

It's also important to me that we stop making assumptions about what young people of any race or gender "should" or "should not" be interested in. This argument that girls aren't interested in STEM or making or building is just total nonsense. I have a wait list of one hundred plus girls who will tell you otherwise. Our belief that they aren't interested is our own baggage. Let those girls prove you wrong.

What's the best advice you've been given since starting?
Two things come to mind. The first comes from a mentor of mine, whom I saw at a conference I was speaking at about a year into Project H's existence. I was super nervous, as I had not done much public speaking yet. He

told me, "Just have fun. If you don't have fun, no one else will." This sounds so ridiculously simple and almost lame, but it has stuck with me, particularly anytime I'm working with young people. I am totally committed to challenging, rigorous, creative work that is hard and fulfilling. But I also think that none of that stuff sticks with you unless the experience itself is joyful, positive, and happy. So I try to create experiences for kids, whether we're learning how to weld, or building a greenhouse, or doing architectural drawings, that are challenging, but always fun. What's the point of doing work you love if you aren't able to share it with others in a joyful way?

And second, James Victore sent me a poster that reads: "Freedom is something you take." This is also

It's also important to me that we stop making assumptions about what young people of any race or gender "should" or "should not" be interested in.

great advice for anyone doing work that feels uncomfortable, risky, or outside of the norm. Freedom is so important to me because it gives me the space to experiment and fail, to adapt and be responsive to the needs of others. I try to remember this advice and instill the same feeling in young people.

The notion of community is unique for everyone. How do you experience it in your life?
The word *community* is so big and nebulous and means so many different things at different scales. But for me I think it's a pretty small circle. Community to me is the people you interact with face-to-face, in a place, whose lives you share in some way. My community is my

family, my colleagues, my young builder girls, my students, the partners we build for, and the people who come into our space to contribute something. My community is small and intimate. I think it's the intimacy of my community and the intimacy of our work that make it so meaningful to me.

How has giving back to the community played a role in the work you are doing?
Giving back to the community has really been at the center of all of our work and actually the thing that gives all of the work meaning. The very first session of Girls Garage, summer 2013, I remember preparing for camp, never having worked with young girls in such a focused way before, and wondering how they would feel about building projects for other people. Specifically, we were building furniture for a local women's shelter, which would mean girls would design and build these pieces and then give them away. It was important to me to model the act of using skills for a collective benefit, but I also wondered if some girls would say, "I want to take that home!"

At the end of camp, the girls did written reflections, and nearly every single girl said their favorite part was knowing that the thing they made would be used by other people who needed it. Not one of them said they wished they could keep it, or that they wished they had made some superfluous thing to take home to their parents.

This has also always been the case with the design/build projects we do with high school students: a farmer's market for a small town, a greenhouse for a community garden, tiny homes for the homeless. I actually think that young people in particular are more invested in work that they know will live in the world and serve others.

I think all of us, and especially young people, want to know that we have value and purpose, and what better way to do that than to put your skills to work for others? Giving back to the community is a way of sharing our stories, a source of strength, and blurs the lines of what is ours versus theirs, mine, or yours.

Have you had any conflicts or challenges choosing to have a social impact mission over a traditional bottom-line-driven approach?
The conflicts or challenges have been in the constant redefinition and creation of a nonprofit model that works for us: that allows us to sustain the work financially while pushing the impact socially. Many times those things are at odds: how do you survive as an organization when your mission is to make experiences accessible to those who cannot afford or access them otherwise? But at the end of the day, I believe the key is always partnerships; there are organizations and colleagues and institutions that support our work in so many profound ways. The challenge is always to think about what currency we trade in, because it isn't dollars. We measure our success by how many girls learn how to weld, how many high school students are graduating instead of dropping out, how many parents are now invested in their kids' educations, or how our communities benefit from projects.

What has been your greatest accomplishment to date?
Opening the doors of Girls Garage. Prior to having our own space, we ran all of our youth programs (Studio H, in-school high school design/build class, *and* Girls Garage) out of classroom space within a public school. With the accomplishments of our Studio H program came

this undeniable energy from my female students to help support them in a girls-only program. It wasn't until 2016 that we opened a physical space only for girls, which is a 3,600-square-foot workshop in West Berkeley that houses a wood and metal shop, digital fabrication, and classroom. It's gorgeous and I love going there every day. Everything is organized and colorful and just inspires you to build stuff. But most important, our girls (more than three hundred!) get out of their parents' cars on the curb and walk through a doorway that says Girls Garage above it, past a wall with a laser-etched tile with their name on it, and into a space that they really feel is their own.

What's next for you and your organization?
I feel like the answer most people would give to this question is some version of "We want to do more!" I want to work with as many young people as possible and build amazing things in many communities, but more important than scale or quantity, I want to do better. As we approach our tenth birthday as an organization, I recognize that we're still growing and constantly trying to steer the ship just slightly in order to do better. I hope what's next for us is to go deeper, meaning to work with our young people for more years of their life, to know them and their families even better, and to better measure, document, and share everything we do.

What impact do you hope to have in ten years?
I really hope that in ten years our impact has been a sort of quiet revolution; that it isn't seen as shocking anymore that a group of teenagers would build a farmer's market for their town, or that ten-year-old girls are welding furniture for the women's shelter. I suppose the best impact would be a change in social expectations so that we just assume that everyone is capable of greatness. On a smaller scale, I'd love for Girls Garage to still be open and thriving, and to be a beacon in the community where all girls feel excited and welcome to try something new. And I hope that the young people I know now come back in ten years and share all their life stories with us, and carry the torch.

You can only get so far with you.

However, with a community, your possibilities are endless.

—Antionette Carroll

building strong bodies, inside and out

Two and a half hours north of New York City, a modern black barn sits on a small stretch of grass off of Route 209 in Ulster County. Once home to a pizza restaurant, it now houses a workout space that has become a special and sacred space to women of all ages looking for community, support, and strength.

by Grace Bonney

photographs by Kelly Merchant

anya Miszko Kefer runs 30 Minutes of Everything, a workout system that, as the name suggests, offers up a little bit of everything in half an hour. And while the training is important, it's the woman—and the mission—behind this business that sets it apart from the difficult gym atmospheres to which so many of us have become accustomed.

In an industry dominated by men and complicated attitudes about weight and body image, Tanya has managed to create a business that feels like a home away from home for so many women. I wanted to learn the secret behind her mission and how she built the safe community she did, so we sat down to talk about how 30 Minutes of Everything became the supportive space for physical health it is.

What did you want to be when you were little?

Well, I'm still little, but when I was younger, I wanted to be an American Gladiator. I was so in awe of their strength and the fact that they could do anything.

What was your path to the professional work you do now?

Growing up I was a gymnast, so I was always active. Going to college I knew I wasn't going to be competing anymore, but I wanted to stay in shape. I wanted muscles! I wanted to train like an American Gladiator and be one of them, so I studied exercise science in college. I loved learning about the human body and the effect that exercise has on it, so I went all the way through college to get my doctorate.

I have done private training with clients since I was twenty-one years old. Moving back home to a rural area (Accord, New York) where my private services would be considered a luxury, I needed to figure out how to still do what I love and reach more people. So I opened up a group fitness studio that is currently serving over two hundred people in each eight-week program.

What is your favorite thing about your studio?

I love that there is a lot of peaceful energy in here. That's an oxymoron for a fitness studio, but it's true.

Tanya Miszko Kefer

What was the best piece of business advice you were given when you were starting off?

Many people told me that you needed to start *big* and go all in. Not being a risk taker, I was scared to death. So I didn't start big. I did it slowly, over time, and I am so glad that I did. It gave me time to learn how to manage my business and my clients and to grow into the businessperson I wanted to be.

What is the biggest sacrifice you've made in starting or running your business?

Sadly, probably my marriage. I love what I do, and it's my number one passion. I spend so many hours creating programs and brainstorming how to make things better. But I need to learn when to stop working and when to just be still. I'm not good at that. I'm working on it.

What does success mean to you?

Happiness. For me, success has never been about money. It's always about doing what I was meant to do and helping as many people as I can. When someone tells me how their life has changed because of their participation in my program, that fills my heart. That is my version of success.

Name a fear or professional challenge that still keeps you up at night.

That someone "better" will come along. The fitness field changes so quickly and I have to constantly be learning and reading to stay current. It's a lot of pressure.

What is your favorite part of your job?

Sharing a moment with my clients when they tell me how the program has helped their daily life. It can be small or big, but it's a positive change to their life. I love to know that what they're doing in the studio is transferring to what they do outside the studio. I'm making a difference and I love that.

You've created a community that is body positive, noncompetitive, and supportive (which is rare in the fitness world). How did you cultivate that and was it something you wanted to create from the start?

I love that about the studio. I feel that the atmosphere is a mix of me and the people inside the studio. Growing up in a gymnastics leotard, I was always the "bigger" girl on the team but most often always the strongest. I've personally grown into my own body and embraced how it's strong and powerful, and *that* is what matters, not the size of my jeans. I just want everyone to love themselves and to be strong and feel good about their bodies. Since the beginning, I've wanted my studio to be for every *body,* every human. I wanted everyone to be comfortable in my studio. No one should be excluded from feeling great and getting healthy.

Do you have to continually stay on top of the tone and vibe of your classes and students to maintain this atmosphere?

Not at all! People who are looking for a half-naked fitness coach won't find that here. They know they can roll out of bed and come to class in their pajamas with no makeup on and we're not going to judge them. No one is going to care. The studio is body positive and there's really no other option.

Name the biggest overall lesson you've learned in running a business.

Don't ever stop learning about your field and working on yourself. Staying current in any field is important and that gives me an advantage over someone who gets comfortable in their business.

How has learning from a mistake ever led to success for you? Walk us through that.

My husband and I had another business before I opened my studio. We sunk every dollar and cashed in my retirement to start it and fund it. That put us in debt from day one. We had no safety net. Because businesses don't always run smoothly and something always comes up, we got into even more debt.

There were days where we couldn't pay any of our bills and I was so afraid. I had never been in that situation before. I had my first anxiety attack at thirty-nine years old and thought I was having a heart attack. While that business was sucking the life out of me, I was also starting my other business (my studio).

Never wanting to start behind the eight ball ever again, I vowed that I would do whatever I needed to do so my studio didn't have debt. I saw clients before I went to my other job at 6 a.m., sometimes on lunch breaks, and on weekends. I busted my butt to raise the money to build my studio and get started without debt. It took me two years to save up enough money, but I did it! Never again will I be in that situation.

In moments of self-doubt or adversity, how do you build yourself back up?

I read my devotionals or listen to a podcast from my online church. That resets me and gets my head and heart back on track, every time.

What are you most proud of in your business experience so far?

I am most proud of how many people in my small town trust me with their health that they've been with my program for years. They keep signing up. Attrition is typically high in fitness studios, but my clients have created such an amazing community that no one wants to leave!

What does the world need more of? Less of?

More tolerance for individual differences. We're all different human beings with the same basic needs. Less selfishness and more selflessness would be great, too! So many people could benefit from others' kindness and generosity.

What is your no-fail go-to when you need inspiration or to get out of a rut?

A walk on this little strip of country road whose backdrop is lush green trees and mountains. It has an amazing view and always puts a smile on my face. It reminds me of how beautiful my town is and how fortunate I am to be here.

In a world where women receive so many negative messages about their bodies, how do you counteract that in your gym?

I try to reinforce to women that they are more than just a body. Who they are isn't dependent upon how much they weigh or the stretch marks on their bodies. I don't have a scale in my studio, nor do I emphasize body weight. I make a point to talk about someone's personal character strengths to remind them of how special they are.

artwork by Robert & Stella

IT DOESN'T

MATTER WHERE

YOU COME FROM

WE ALL DESERVE

TO DREAM

— Bethany Yellowtail

break down and break through

Writer and public affairs specialist Heather Barmore discusses the importance of communicating mental health needs at home and at work.

by Heather L. Barmore

illustrations by Loveis Wise

"So! I quit my job!"

My enthusiasm left hanging in the air for a bit until a response.

"What do you mean 'quit'?" Said with a sharp emphasis on the "t."

I sighed. "I mean that I had a massive anxiety attack and while lying in the middle of my apartment, covered in tears, I told my boss that I just couldn't do it anymore. I couldn't go to work. I couldn't come back. I was done."

"Oh . . ."

"Yeah. . . ."

"Well, it happens," and a shrug.

No, it doesn't "just happen."

It doesn't happen to people with normal serotonin levels, those who don't spend an hour each month discussing mood-stabilizers and medication adjustments.

It doesn't happen to people who don't carry benzodiazepines in their back pockets, front pockets, and three purses because anxiety can strike at the most inopportune moments.

It doesn't happen to people who don't find themselves physically unable to get to work. Do you know how many times I have texted a supervisor about a generic stomach issue with an emoji frown face?

It doesn't "just happen."

The short and dirty history of my mental health, because context helps:

2002 On the outside, I am a regular college student in Washington, DC. During the day I intern on Capitol Hill and absorb the information from courses called Politics of the Civil Rights Movement and Advanced Macroeconomics. At night, I walk around my DC neighborhood and extinguish lit cigarettes on my arms, just to feel something. It's suggested that I am depressed, and I am referred to a therapist whom I spend a year (and several thousand dollars) just staring at during appointments. I don't want to talk to a stranger about why my burnt flesh is the only thing that makes me feel as if I'm actually alive.

2007 My depression has turned into incontrollable rage. Anything and everything sets me off. I scream at friends; I throw things. A friend suggests Xanax and, as if flipping a switch, I am able to calm down. I become less frantic and unclench my jaw, long enough to visit a psychiatrist who diagnoses me with Bipolar II disorder. It's a name and names are good. A name is a tangible thing to point to and to research. I am put on a cocktail of medication and subjected to once-a-month blood draws to check my Lithium levels.

2009 During a bout of depression, I am about to take an exit and casually wonder what might happen if I drive my car off of an overpass. This time I am able to recognize that this is not normal. Progress! I get a bit more Lexapro in me and we're good to go.

Work is shit. My boss is toxic. My former roommate is making attempts to get me fired (spoiler alert: she eventually succeeds). I send apology texts to friends and family and ingest the entirety of my psych meds and yet I manage to wake up the following morning. I'm groggy but otherwise perfectly fine.

I am back in Washington, DC, working in an office situated between the White House and the Trump Hotel. I am anxious all of the time. The anxiety leads to terrible, regular stomachaches, which I mention to my psychiatrist, who tells me he is having a hard time diagnosing anxiety these days ("Is it real anxiety or is it this overwhelming news cycle?"). He sounds a bit depressed as well. Regardless, an epiphany, I have severe Generalized Anxiety Disorder and Unipolar Depression, not bipolar. Again, with names and diagnoses, things begin to fall into place. I am given a prescription for a hefty dose of benzodiazepines.

Despite the benzos, stress leads to a massive anxiety attack. I scream. I claw at my clothing. I am in the middle of my apartment floor unable to complete a cohesive sentence to my boss, the chief of staff to a big city mayor, except for: "I can't do it. I can't do it anymore."

When you admit to being a person with a severe mental illness,

you are able to come up to the surface a bit and gasp,

able to see what is around, knowing that somewhere nearby there is someone to bring you to shore.

In my resignation letter, I give effusive praise and apologies in between painfully brutal, possibly career-ending honesty:

"I had an anxiety attack and abdicated my responsibilities."

"I should have been more honest about my mental health."

"Mental health issues are as debilitating as physical health issues, and my only regret is not telling you sooner."

In writing these words and making these admissions, I find myself for once able to talk about my mental illness without embarrassment or shame, just relief.

When you're consistently, constantly anxious, it means being unable to breathe.

I liken it to swimming.

At first, I am casually doing a breaststroke, feeling myself glide through the chlorinated water, until, without notice, I feel sudden fatigue, which quickly gives way to attempting to push forward to no avail. I am physically unable to move. I allow myself to sink wondering if I'll ever be able to come up for air.

When you admit to being a person with a severe mental illness, you are able to come up to the surface a bit and gasp, able to see what is around, knowing that somewhere nearby there is someone to bring you to shore.

For every story of a woman able to say to her coworkers that she is taking time off to take care of her mental health, there are those like me: we hide, hope, pretend. Everything is always okay.

By day, I am "on," shaking hands, speaking in complete sentences. The end of the day arrives and, like clockwork, I must retreat from the world. I put my phones on do not disturb with periodic checks because my anxiety tells me that at some point at some time in the evening there will be an emergency. I want to be needed and capable, but I also want to hide from the world.

Here's the thing: how do you tell an employer that you are mentally ill?

Just casually drop it in the opening paragraph of the cover letter? Add it to your résumé? Is it during the initial interview? "Hi! I'm Heather! I have contemplated suicide on more than one occasion and I am always and forever so anxious that my whole body aches! It's such a pleasure to meet you!" Or do you just wait for them to find out as you fall, spectacularly, into pieces, on your apartment floor with body-wracking sobs, unable to breathe due to your anxiety?

When is the best time to mention to your colleagues that you cannot control your brain?

How?

When?

No one knows about the physical part of mental illness. The way in which it sabotages your ability to get through the day. The way in which you compare yourself with your coworkers. It's not just, "Oh, Susan! You're so organized!" It's more like, "Oh! Susan! How do you go about your day *not* feeling as if your brain will cause you to spin wildly out of control?"

What is that like?

Several weeks later I relay this story to a former colleague. "Why didn't you say anything? Why didn't you tell me?"

In 2002, I would have said that I was embarrassed. Now? Now it's because there is no easy way to tell someone that you are mentally ill except to, well, just say it. You can't hide it. You can't pray the mental illness away. You just accept it as if you would accept any other physical illness, except this one won't manifest itself in a visual change others can see. It is literally all in your head.

There is no amount of hoping that the stigma around mental illness will be erased until first confessing to your own struggles.

There is no amount of hoping that the stigma around mental illness will be erased until first confessing to your own struggles.

October 2017 — I have a new job. And my new boss wants to know about our expectations as employees. I write the following:

"I have unipolar depression. I will need to take days off."

"I have a standing twice-monthly doctor appointment."

"I have generalized anxiety disorder."

"I am always anxious."

"Sometimes I like my door closed because it makes me feel safe."

"I like to write about my mental health to make people feel less alone. I hope you get a chance to read it."

If you or someone you know is in need of resources for mental illness, the following websites, apps, and hotlines are available.

WEBSITES

National Alliance on Mental Illness
www.nami.org

7 Cups
www.7cups.com
free online counseling and listings for local
therapy resources

APPS

Breathe2Relax
a free stress management app that helps with
breathing to reduce stress and anxiety

PTSD Coach
a free app for those who have, or think they
may have, post-traumatic stress disorder

HOTLINES

Crisis Call Center
800-273-8255

Crisis Text Line
a free 24/7 confidential text message service
for people in crisis (text HOME to 741-741
from anywhere in the United States, anytime,
about any type of crisis)

GLBT National Help Center
888-843-4564

LGBT National Youth Talkline
800-246-PRIDE (800-246-7743)

National Crime Victim Helpline
800-FYI-CALL (800-394-2255)

National Domestic Violence Hotline
800-656-HOPE (800-799-7223)

National Sexual Assault Hotline
800-799-SAFE (800-656-4673)

National Suicide Prevention Lifeline
800-273-TALK (800-273-8255)

The Samaritans Crisis Hotline
212-673-3000

Trans Lifeline
877-565-8860

2-1-1
dial for local emergencies in any area

REP
RES
ENT
ED

Writer, teacher,
and disability advocate
Rebekah G. Taussig
explores disability
as an identity and
the importance
of representation.

by Rebekah G. Taussig

illustrations by Maia Boakye

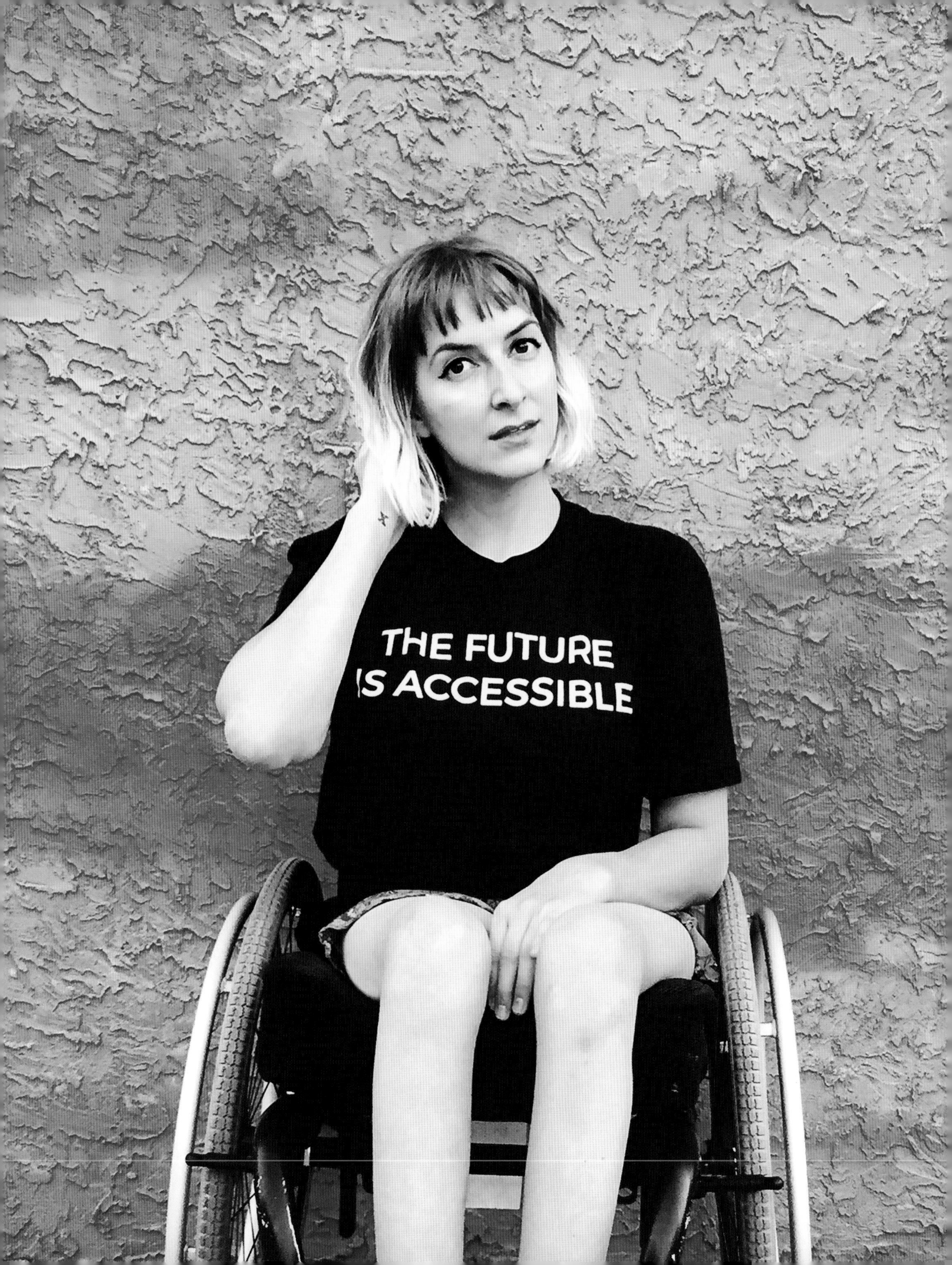
THE FUTURE
IS ACCESSIBLE

This fall I started teaching a disability and literature class to a group of high school seniors. I'd been dreaming of teaching a course like this for years, but now it was real. In the early weeks of the semester, I showed up with my visibly disabled body—scrawny legs resting on the footplate of my wheelchair—lesson plans lined up, eager to pour all the knowledge into their young brains. My enthusiasm was checked by an overwhelming sense of apathy. I was stunned when students couldn't immediately fathom how studying disability literature might be worth their time.

Every weekday since the start of September we've been reading stories and watching films that include characters with bodies and minds that don't fit typical expectations for "normal," and I ask, "What does it mean that this character would rather die than live in his impaired body? Can you think of an example of disabled characters in successful, romantic relationships? No? What are the broader implications of these representations?" These kids were born into the twenty-first century. They've known that diversity is good and discrimination is bad since they were babies. Yeah, yeah, yeah, we get it. Don't be mean to disabled people! We should all be equal! But can these ideas possibly feel more tangible or pressing to them than points on a presentation slide?

They know the "right" answers before I ask the questions, but how do we get to the territory beyond the "right" answers?—how do we step into the space of another person's breathtaking experience?—how do we absorb the sharp pain that comes when someone believes through their spine and into their digits that they do not belong? I wish it were possible to take my high school seniors on a field trip to Manhattan, Kansas, in 1992. They'd file down the stairs of our early-twentieth-century house into the musty basement and find my six-year-old self curled up on the threadbare burgundy velvet sofa, watching my grandma's VHS-taped soap operas. My legs are strapped into clunky metal braces with brown velcro, and my knees are scabby from crawling around the neighborhood. As I sit on that sofa in the basement, picking at my scabs, eyes glued to the sexy scenes of *As the World Turns,* I learn which bodies are desirable. As I grow up, every piece of storytelling, from the news to ads in magazines to *The Little Mermaid,* teaches me where my lopsided body fits. Without asking questions, my little brain observes; thousands upon thousands of images of love and femininity, romance and success, motherhood and power, independence and adulthood flash across my developing brain, and none of them look like me. I wonder if my students would be able to track my growing shame, watch me slowly disappear, more and more disconnected from the world and myself.

By the time I reached adolescence, I had no idea how to imagine myself as any kind of successful adult. There's an eerie entry in my thirteen-year-old diary, where I describe my future. I wrote pages of tedious details painting a picture of myself in my early twenties. In this world, I lived in a very chic apartment and had a high-pressure but creatively fulfilling job, amazing hair, and a boyfriend I named Nathan, who took me out to dinner and made me sweet-smelling bubble baths.

One unaccountable detail in this imagined world is that I am living this posh life with a nondisabled body.

No wheelchairs or braces or feet dragging or accessible transportation or housing accommodations appear anywhere. In fact, the opposite is true. My body fits perfectly into the able-bodied world. I visualized a future body that could slide right into the scenes of adulthood I'd seen performed by Jennifer Aniston or Julia Roberts or Meg Ryan. But imagining my body as gracefully walking makes about

Theorists, writers, artists, and activists that have flipped my world

Sue Austin Multimedia artist who makes stunning videos of scuba diving in her wheelchair. Watch her TED Talk video, "Deep Sea Diving . . . in a Wheelchair," for a glimpse of her work.

Eli Clare Author of *Exile and Pride*. Storyteller, activist, theorist, and poet who explores the intersections of disability, race, gender, sexuality, and class.

Erin Clark Self-created sex-icon, artist, and wheelchair pole-dancer, Erin writes and takes selfies that document her larger-than-life existence. @erinunleashes

Katherine Dunn Author of *Geek Love*, which flips traditional hierarchies, crafting a world where circus freaks have all the power.

Rosemarie Garland-Thomson Author of *Extraordinary Bodies*. One of the founding voices in disability studies.

Lucy Grealy Author of *Autobiography of a Face*. American poet and memoirist who wrote the story of her lifelong pursuit to correct her facial deformities through reconstructive surgeries.

Sonya Huber Author of *Pain Woman Takes Your Keys*. Disabled creative nonfiction writer and professor who turns her chronic pain into lyric essays.

Alison Kafer Author of *Feminist, Queer, Crip*. Theorist who writes stunning prose critically examining the relationship between disability and pop culture, current social and political events, and theoretical constructs.

Bhavna Mehta Visual artist who creates paper and embroidery sculptures around disabled bodies. @bhavnaumehta

Aimee Mullins Athlete, supermodel, and activist who navigates the world on two prosthetic legs and sees her physical impairment as an opportunity for imagination. Her TED Talks, "The Opportunity of Adversity" and "My Twelve Pairs of Legs," are worth watching.

Susan Nussbaum Author of *Good Kings, Bad Kings*, one of the only pieces of fiction narrated by a collection of disabled characters.

Annie Segarra Artist, activist, YouTuber, and creator of the "The Future Is Accessible" T-shirt line. @annieelainey

Andrew Solomon Author of *Far from the Tree*. Nonfiction writer and activist who follows his own open-handed curiosity to explore the intersections between marginalized identities.

Annika Victoria Vivacious, disabled, twentysomething artist who blogs and YouTubes about life and her creative projects: annikavictoria.com @littlepineneedle

Eleanor Wheeler Teenage activist and creator of the We Exist Collective. @elliewheels

Stella Young Revolutionary activist who coined the concept of "inspiration porn" in her TED Talk video, "I'm Not Your Inspiration, Thank You Very Much."

as much sense as picturing my future self as a bird or a houseplant. This had never and would never be a part of my future, but this is the picture I sketched. Why? I wonder: did I not know how to imagine my disabled body into the narratives I found the most enticing? I wanted love and beauty and excitement and fulfillment—all of it—and I didn't see my body creating that kind of life.

How do you explain the power of seeing your own unique form represented in a story to people who've never felt the comprehensive absence of it? No matter how tightly I squinted my eyes, I couldn't see myself becoming any kind of acceptable adult. It sounds dramatic, doesn't it? But I didn't know what kind of work my body could do, how I would find a place to live where I could navigate on my own, how I'd ever afford the insurance to pay for my medical expenses, who would ever be willing to love me. The pieces that seemed automatic, essential, assumed for everyone else seemed impossibly out of reach for me. I'm guessing that when you grow up surrounded by stories that reflect you, it's easier to believe that your dreams for yourself are entirely your own. Why would you notice that the path is already paved when your journey across it is so smooth? By the time I was twenty-two, I'd married the first boy who had shown interest in me, dropped out of school, and given up on any vision for the unique contribution I might bring to the world. As I saw it, being taken care of by a person willing to marry me—a person I loved as a friend, if not as a partner—was the only way I could survive.

We need representation for disabled people for the benefit of those same people, but it's more than that, too. A couple of weeks ago, a few of my students did presentations on the history of institutionalizing disabled people. They described the practice of relegating these bodies into faraway buildings where we could close the door and forget they existed—a collective physical erasure of an entire group. We've exiled these voices from our stories, too—blotted out a vibrant part of our humanity. When I push for more disability representation, part of my motive stems from a desire for disabled people to see themselves as valid participants in culture. But non-disabled people need these stories, too.

A fundamental piece of our human experience is missing when disabled stories are ignored.

These stories are a part of us, whether we acknowledge them or not—they add texture and depth, curiosity and nuance to our understanding of what it means to live a human life on this planet. We are all in desperate need of these stories. All of us.

So, how do we step into this unexplored space? How do we understand the power of representation and begin to feel the weight of its absence? Over the past few months, my students and I have been paying attention. We call out the absence of representation, and we identify where it's skewed. We find the counter-narratives, and we take note. Or, this is what I hope we do. The curiosity, the urgency, has not yet caught us all. But as I assign the work, as we push through the motions each day, as we examine the stories, pay attention, open our minds, and listen, I'm seeing us change—ideas click into place— bit by little bit. This is the power of stepping into stories and tuning in to the voices that have been hushed. If you're interested in doing this kind of work, too, I've included on page 165 a messy pile of resources that have changed me in one way or another. Some of this we've read/watched as a class, and the rest of it I wish we had time to read/watch as a class. My hope is that as we seek out these voices and draw them into our minds and communities, their insights will wash over us, change the way we look at, evaluate, and categorize each other, prompting us to question our methods of determining human worth. I believe there is a better—a kinder, more supportive, creative—version of us out there, and listening to these voices is one way to get there.

artwork and poem by Areeba Siddique

YOU AREN'T TOO MUCH
OR TOO LITTLE
OR A "TOO" AT ALL

YOU'RE A PERFECT BALANCE

OF FIRE, WATER, AIR
& EARTH

MIXED TOGETHER.

Good Company Crossword #1

Legendary members
and moments from our
creative community.

by Meg Mateo Ilasco

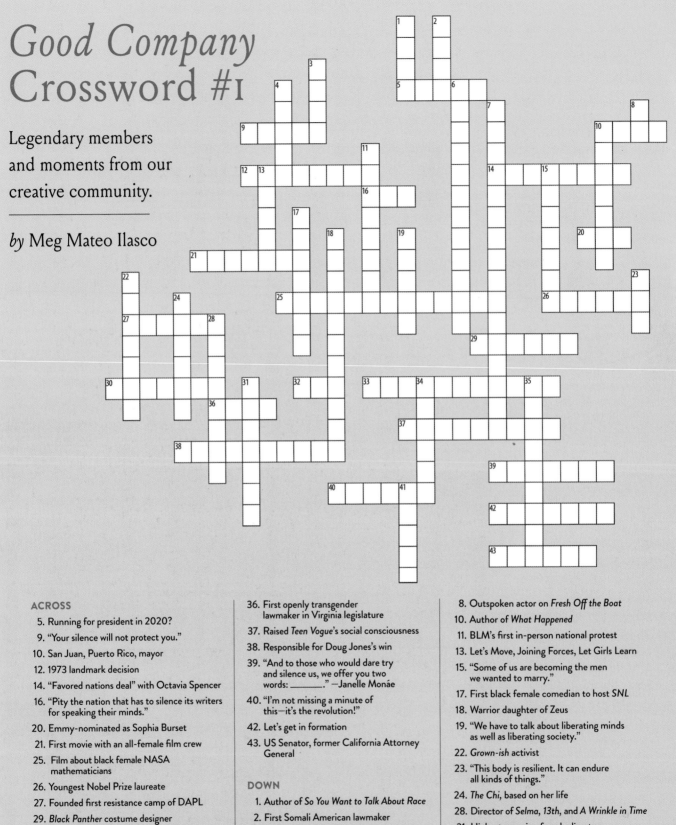

ACROSS

5. Running for president in 2020?
9. "Your silence will not protect you."
10. San Juan, Puerto Rico, mayor
12. 1973 landmark decision
14. "Favored nations deal" with Octavia Spencer
16. "Pity the nation that has to silence its writers for speaking their minds."
20. Emmy-nominated as Sophia Burset
21. First movie with an all-female film crew
25. Film about black female NASA mathematicians
26. Youngest Nobel Prize laureate
27. Founded first resistance camp of DAPL
29. *Black Panther* costume designer
30. "The Danger of a Single Story"
32. "Asian actors should play Asian roles."
33. Are there at least two women talking to each other about something other than a man?
36. First openly transgender lawmaker in Virginia legislature
37. Raised *Teen Vogue*'s social consciousness
38. Responsible for Doug Jones's win
39. "And to those who would dare try and silence us, we offer you two words: _____." —Janelle Monáe
40. "I'm not missing a minute of this—it's the revolution!"
42. Let's get in formation
43. US Senator, former California Attorney General

DOWN

1. Author of *So You Want to Talk About Race*
2. First Somali American lawmaker
3. _____ *and Thea: A Very Long Engagement*
4. #MeToo movement creator
6. Afro-Latinx reality star speaks on colorism
7. Garza, Tometi, and Cullors
8. Outspoken actor on *Fresh Off the Boat*
10. Author of *What Happened*
11. BLM's first in-person national protest
13. Let's Move, Joining Forces, Let Girls Learn
15. "Some of us are becoming the men we wanted to marry."
17. First black female comedian to host *SNL*
18. Warrior daughter of Zeus
19. "We have to talk about liberating minds as well as liberating society."
22. *Grown-ish* activist
23. "This body is resilient. It can endure all kinds of things."
24. *The Chi*, based on her life
28. Director of *Selma*, *13th*, and *A Wrinkle in Time*
31. Highest-grossing female director
34. Sí se puede
35. First Latinx on the High Bench
41. #OscarSoWhite original tweet

ANSWERS: See designsponge.com/crossword.